DRIVING
THE DATA

DRIVING
THE DATA

HOW YOU CAN
DREAM, BUY, AND
THRIVE IN THE
PROPERTY MARKET

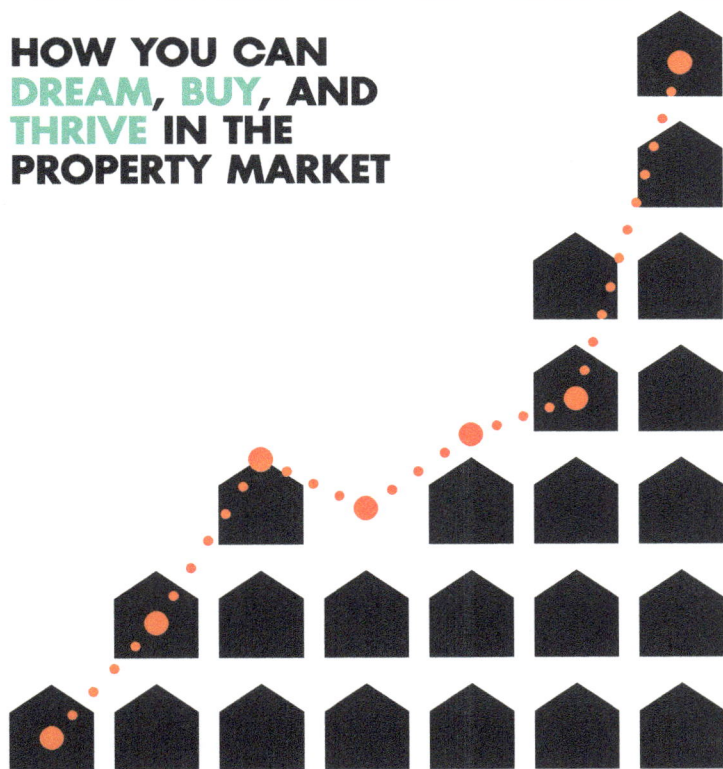

ARJUN PALIWAL

First published in 2025 by Dean Publishing

DEAN PUBLISHING

PO Box 119
Mt. Macedon, Victoria, 3441
Australia
deanpublishing.com

Title: Driving The Data
ISBN: 978-0-648995-73-9
Category: Business/Real Estate

Printed in Australia
Text design by Publish Central
Text additions by Dean Publishing
Cover design by Julia Kuris

CONTENTS

Preface   The day that stopped me in my tracks   vii

Part I: Myth busting   1

Chapter 1   To learn we must unlearn   3
Chapter 2   Myths about strategy   9
Chapter 3   Myths about location and trends   25
Chapter 4   Myths about the property   37
Chapter 5   Myths about tools and indicators   49
Chapter 6   Myths about opportunities   61

TL:DR 3 tips   70

Part II: Fundamentals   71

Chapter 7   What are the property fundamentals?   73
Chapter 8   Demand   77
Chapter 9   Supply   93
Chapter 10   Confidence   101

TL:DR 3 tips   114

Part III: Market categorisation frameworks   117

Chapter 11   Unlearning the property clock   119
Chapter 12   Early-adopter markets   137
Chapter 13   Hotspot markets   149
Chapter 14   Second-wind markets   161

TL:DR 3 tips   171

Part IV: Acquisition and due diligence   **173**

Chapter 15   Understanding the research   175
Chapter 16   The dangers of getting this wrong   179
Chapter 17   The 20-point due diligence checklist   183
Chapter 18   The grey areas   191
Chapter 19   Success stories   197

TL:DR 3 tips   204

Epilogue   205
About the Author   209

THE DAY THAT STOPPED ME IN MY TRACKS

It was the day that stopped me in my tracks. A true day of reckoning that changed everything.

It was 10 am one morning in April 2024 when I heard a knock on my front door. Standing there on my porch was a police officer.

'I'm looking for Arjun Paliwal,' the officer said.

I'd never in my life had any reason to be in touch with the police, and before I'd had a chance to process, I blurted out:

'Oh my god. What the actual frick have I done?!'

'I'm here because I wanted to check that you're alive,' he said.

Come again?! I'm here, alive and very well, I thought. I had recently had some tests done for a new life insurance policy. Perhaps it was about that.

'I'm doing a welfare check.'

'What for?' I said.

'Your doctor is extremely concerned that something has happened to you, because you're not picking up his phone calls.'

That much was true, I admitted.

'Sorry, I'm non-stop. Busy, busy, busy!' I exclaimed.

'Well, you need to call your doctor ASAP.'

In those few minutes, the life I knew and loved began to look and feel very different. I had a wife, Leigh, and a little girl, Ruby, who was one. It dawned on me that for a police officer to show up on my doorstep to tell me to see my doctor things must be pretty serious. I began to sense that something was very wrong.

The police officer left and I rang my doctor immediately, and yes, sure enough, they said I needed to go in ASAP.

The next day, I heard the news that became both my nightmare and my saviour.

My doctor told me I had an extremely serious heart condition. He explained that a normal heart's left ventricular diameter is 45 to 55 mm. If you have a left ventricular diameter 55 to 60 mm or more, you're incredibly at risk and require urgent medical attention.

Mine was 73 mm.

And I was in the 1% of people in Australia who has what's called a 'leaking bicuspid aortic valve'. Apparently, it's the hardest-working valve in the heart, and mine just happened to be leaking. This means that my heart swells like the underside of a cabinet when it gets wet, doing double the outflow work of the other valves to compensate for the blood leaking out.

My heart leakage was so severe that the doctor sat and stared at me as though I was some kind of medical marvel.

'I don't quite know how you're breathing and standing,' he said. 'Your body has adjusted to this condition – it's miraculous.'

He then told me I needed open-heart surgery as soon as possible and that my life expectancy had dropped to a few years.

Wow.

I felt nothing like a medical marvel. I felt numb, confused and scared, but I knew deep down I needed to have this surgery. Not only did I need to help my heart but also ensure my family would have me around for as long as possible.

What transpired next was a whirlwind of researching the best procedures, specialists and hospitals. I found out that the heart condition was something I was born with, and that my ventricular diameter needed to reduce to under 60 mm for me to be out of the danger zone.

In one month, I found the only specialist in Australia in Melbourne, with an impressive track record and who could carry out the surgery I needed, which involved not one operation on my valve but two, and a surgery duration double the time of a standard open-heart operation. I'd be on the table for up to eight hours.

It's called the 'Ross Procedure', and it involves removing the aortic valve altogether and taking the pulmonary valve nearby and placing it in the aortic position. The aim is to use my own body parts instead of introducing foreign elements, such as the more commonly used cow or pig valves, enhancing the body's chance of acceptance.

The operation involves a second component where a valve is used in the pulmonary position, from a human donation. Ultimately, the procedure would give me up to 20 to 40 years of life instead of 8 to 10 before another operation is needed.

I was booked in for surgery the following week.

My wife and family offered their unconditional support, which was made a little easier because they all live with us. We are a happy family of 13, living on a five-acre block in Pitt Town, Sydney, across two houses. In one house, there's me, Leigh, Ruby and our latest addition Amir, plus my brother, his wife and their sons, Ari and Armaan. In the second house lives my dad, step-mum, stepsister, mother-in-law and sister-in-law. It's true intergenerational living, and the reason I work so hard – so I can provide for the most treasured people in my life.

Up until that point, I had worked tirelessly all day every day to build the world around me, being able to provide an incredible home and support my family and extended family.

But this turn of events did cause me to start questioning everything.

LIVING LIFE TO THE FULLEST

I've always been about striving high and living life to the fullest. I've an insatiable curiosity – a sense of what could be possible – and I can see that everything I've done in my 33 years has been fuelled by these things.

I was born in Wellington, New Zealand, and moved to Australia on Guy Fawkes Day when I was 18, in 2010. I used to be a male model for HOYTs cinema and was even a pro dancer with the Sydney Krump Community. I played basketball in high school with some heavy hitters, including against Steven Adams who is now New Zealand's best basketballer and a star in the NBA.

As for work, I struggled when I moved to Australia. I couldn't land a job for many months. My first role was as a bank teller at CBA in Parramatta, in 2011. I loved numbers and finance and seeing all the success of my clients – as well as the mistakes they made, which I could learn from. Most of all, I loved the possibilities of where my career could go and what I could do to make a positive impact on the banking world.

Before long, I became one of Australia's youngest branch managers at 21 years old, earning six figures and winning the prestigious CEO Award. I achieved the highest status in CBA.

Working at the bank also piqued another curiosity – for property. One day a client came in who had a few investment properties. I was looking after his banking, and the curiosity was killing me. I just had to ask …

'How did you do it?'

He told me he was a buyers' agent. Ummm …. what's that?

From that point, I was hooked. I studied everything I could get my hands on and learned how successful investors thought and markets operated. I started to unravel the volatile world of the property market, where, as well as the success stories, there were also huge mistakes by investors, like buying an apartment because they thought they couldn't afford a house, only buying in their backyard, relying on E-valuation platforms or ignoring the importance of due diligence.

After serious research and hard work, I eventually felt confident enough to buy my first property for $970,000. I was 22 and I purchased it with my wife, Leigh. It was in Glenwood, Sydney, in 2015 – halfway through a major boom. This first place was a house to live in, but we eventually changed it to an investment and became rentvestors. Fast forward to today, we own our dream home.

After that I engaged a buyers' agent, who helped me purchase more properties. One was successful, while the others were very low performers and resulted in both time and financial losses. I acquired a couple of properties before COVID and sold them during the boom for roughly the same amounts I had purchased them for. I was not a part of the boom for those two properties.

I got burnt.

This taught me a lot. It hasn't been all smooth sailing for me – property teaches you a thing or two along the way, and while that first Glenwood property did well, I thought there had to be more. I also thought people should get better results when working with a buyers' agent.

So I decided to get serious. Well, *more* serious. I returned to study to further grow my income and career, basically working around the clock with five hours' sleep and either work or study in between. I graduated with my MBA from the Australian Institute of Business, and through the grind secured a strategy and research role in CBA's head office.

I also finally felt confident to buy my next investment property, in Burnie, Tasmania, for $365,000, at a time when no one considered buying there.

In just five years, the value of that property doubled to $785,000. After some renovations of about $130,000 in 2022, it's now worth over $1.1 million and rents for over $1,200 per week.

By age 25 (2018), Leigh and I owned nine properties (eight residential and one commercial). Now, at the age of 33, I've purchased 17 properties in various suburbs across Australia. I bought all of these properties sight unseen, except for my own home. I'm humbled to have a portfolio value of $17 million at the time of writing.

With hindsight, I can see now that hearing the news from my doctor was my saviour. It was true that it had only come about because of the extra health tests I had to do because business was good and I needed more insurance, but I still wouldn't want anyone to go through hearing that news.

THE BEGINNING OF INVESTORKIT

Back in 2018 – the year I owned nine investment properties – I had a revelation.

I was mid-flight from Bali. I had quit my job after eight years in banking, and was taking some time off. Call it a pre-mid-life crisis! As a leading finance broker, Leigh had stayed at work, and I had quit with an inkling that I could create my own business but wasn't sure how or what that looked like.

While away, I had time to reflect. I realised how many people were seeking my guidance on property investing and I thought I could do a better job at residential investing than the buyers' agent I had used, with my unique focus on market research and timing.

Then it hit me. Why didn't I start a business as a buyers' agent?

Not long after, I established InvestorKit, and the only way was up. From humble beginnings, I grew the business with a vision to create a data-driven and battle-tested process for busy professionals to invest with confidence and build their wealth by outperforming the market.

I'm so proud of our achievements:

- seven consecutive years of 50%+ growth as a business
- 2,000+ properties purchased
- $1 billion+ in real estate experience
- $500 million+ in equity growth for our clients
- Outperformed the national market by over 49%
- 1,000+ clients helped.

Plus, a whole bunch of incredible awards, including:

- Australia's Buyer's Agency of the Year 2023 and 2024, by Real Estate Business (we are the first company to achieve this)
- Real Estate Business 2020 Rising Star
- Finalist Young Entrepreneur of the Year for Sydney 2021, 2022 and 2023, by Business News Australia
- one of the Top 10 places to work by *The Australian* 2024 for teams with less than 50 employees
- Top 50 Small Business Leader by Inside Small Business 2022
- Top 100 Young Small Business Entrepreneur by Business News Australia (ranked 71st)
- Australia's 18th fastest growing SME 2024 by Smart Company.

WHO THIS BOOK IS FOR AND HOW TO READ IT

I've always wanted to write a book, and when I was told that my life might be over in a few short years, it gave me a reinvigorated energy to get it done sooner than later.

Following a successful operation and my ventricular size decreasing, I'm not out of the woods, but I look at life through a fresh – healthier – lens, and that's a wonderful way to be. I've changed physically and emotionally, but my passion for helping people build their legacy for their families by blocking out all the noise to make data-driven decisions has never erred.

We all bring biases, family 'advice' and fear-mongering from the media to the property table. But you can't argue with evidence or numbers, which makes what we do so different and compelling. We don't believe in luck – we believe in research, diligence and clarity. It's irrefutable.

And of course, we believe in curiosity.

So, if you're a busy professional or successful business owner who wants to scale your portfolio – *this book is for you.*

If you're in the middle of the corporate ladder and killing it in your career – *this book is for you.*

If you value professional guidance, building a team and are time-poor – *this book is for you.*

If you want to grow an impressive seven- or eight-figure property portfolio backed by data – *this book is for you.*

Most of all, if you strive to create a legacy for your children, providing them with a financial stepping stone for their future – *this book is especially for you.*

Let's go!

PART I
MYTH BUSTING

Now that you know my story, it's time to tune into yours. Because everybody has a story about property.

Property serves as an incredible vehicle for many purposes – from fulfilling the basic human right to shelter to realising dreams as a multi-property investor. Hopefully, this is why you're reading this book.

While we all have stories about property, most of these are founded on and fuelled by mistruths, myths and so-called 'facts' from media with an agenda or publications to sell, or friends and family who place thoughts in your head rent-free that become solid beliefs.

The truth is that only 10% of Australian individual investors own three or more investment properties. That means there are 90% who don't, and who haven't gone through the process of building a portfolio and therefore possibly don't understand what's really going on in the property market.

That 90% believe in things like buying blue-chip properties, buying only in capital cities, buying near the best schools or cities or beach, and using your maximum budget.

But they're wrong. I'm going to show you why. This section is all about how this approach won't take you to where you want to be. I will take you through the most common myths so you can unlearn them, and then we will go back to property basics and fundamentals later in the book.

Chapter 1

TO LEARN WE MUST UNLEARN

The whole concept of myths came up for me when I realised how popular the most commonly held property 'beliefs' are in Australia. Think about it: we often inherit the way we think about homes, investing and the property market from our parents or those closest to us.

My approach is data-driven. I've spent the last 10-plus years studying the numbers and building my portfolio based on data, not opinion. After all, how many times have you picked up a property book and read about a new investing tactic with little to back it up other than what's written on the page, but asking you to part with your money to have the privilege of learning it?

I'm going to prove to you that almost everything you think you know about property is based on an assumption, and that it doesn't stack up against hard data. It might be hard, uncomfortable and challenging to 'unlearn' some of these assumptions you thought were true, but I want you to start by pressing pause. Knowledge is power, and it all starts with unlearning.

Prepare to be challenged on what you think you know!

THE DIFFERENT INVESTMENT JOURNEYS

Before we go into unlearning the myths, let's start by looking at the three ways most people come into property investing:

1. the accidental investor
2. the common beliefs investor
3. the family investor.

All three pathways may have led to a property investment purchase, but they're often based on ingredients that feel comfortable and places that may look nice and feel nice or that have been recommended by well-meaning but uninformed family members. When you realise how investors in these three types 'fall' into investment, it's not hard to see why their investments don't do as well as they *think* they will or have been *sold* that they will.

The accidental investor

I've included this first because it's essentially how most people become investors: *accidentally*. It works like this: you buy a home to live in, which solves the necessity of housing and shelter. Then, if you decide you want to upsize your home or change location, you turn that first property into an investment property when you acquire your second. By holding on rather than selling, you've inadvertently become an investor. This wasn't your intention when making the purchase, but then changes in income, your family or work situation, or other circumstances arise.

Chances are this property wasn't purchased with the metrics or the data of an investment property. And it was purchased in your backyard. Now you have two properties in the same city: you're a property investor! But will you be a *profitable* property investor?

I'm all for property investment in any form, and if that's how you get onto the ladder, that's fine. But I want to shift the conversation from *accidental* investing to *intentional* investing, because you may not have made a sound, informed investment. And after you've bought, it's too late.

The approach I prefer is to look at the bigger picture. Rather than buying in your backyard, consider the whole of Australia, and use data to make a more intentional decision.

The common beliefs investor

This investor is defined as representing the most common ways people jump into beliefs about property investing. It's the chat at the friend's barbecue about how so-and-so has bought a few places in area X and reckons it's a hotspot. It's reading the weekend paper and identifying a niche stat anchoring an entire article about an area and believing it's an emerging hotspot. It's continually hearing popular beliefs about property and assuming they're fact. One of the biggest is 'location, location, location' – but it's simply not applicable once you apply a rigorous set of metrics.

The family investor

This is a tricky investing type to break. For those lucky enough to have a family to turn to, they can offer us fantastic advice on navigating life and big issues. But family members and relatives are also obliging with well-meaning advice and guidance about where and what to invest your money into, and these are usually investments that feel comfortable, are close to them, and which they presume would make a sound investment.

But our families aren't property investors (well, most of them!). With next to no data as evidence, their 'insight' is probably ill-founded and likely to create a poor-performing investment.

* * *

Whether you recognise yourself in one of these groups or have yet to jump on the property ladder, at some stage you do have to back yourself and stop listening to the noise.

That means putting down the motivational books, stopping the property podcasts (except InvestorKit's podcast, of course!), stopping the 'wealth manifesting', and admitting that maybe you don't know this stuff as well as you should. Especially if you're investing large amounts of money, and what that represents for you.

Instead, get smart and informed so that you can make the best decisions right from the start.

ARJUN'S INSIGHT

You need to learn the craft and not wish the result. Yes, it's okay to have self-belief and a good money mindset, but you still need to have a conversation with yourself to realise that a more informed, intelligent, research-based approach is the right way to invest. I know this can be hard, because you have to put aside the influencing factors in your life and back yourself. *The data won't let you down!*

A great place to start unlearning what you think you know about property is to see how most of the property 'education' you currently believe is not actually true. By busting the most popular myths in the industry, I'll show you why the myths are exactly that, and how you can see past them.

While I love proving these wrong, I also want to present you with the data behind the truth. You can't hide from the black-and-white figures, no matter how much they challenge your thinking.

I've grouped the myths into five categories and chapters:

- *Myths about strategy*
- *Myths about location and trends*
- *Myths about the property*
- *Myths about tools and indicators*
- *Myths about opportunities.*

Let's unlearn!

Chapter 2

MYTHS ABOUT STRATEGY

In books on property investment, property strategy often appears straightforward, shaped by principles of growth, location and market trends. Yet, many myths and misconceptions lurk. Behind the dismissive attitudes, anecdotes, assumptions and outdated models, these myths and misconceptions create a culture where certain beliefs are accepted without scrutiny.

Accepting so-called 'safe bets' without question can mislead even seasoned investors into decisions that overlook emerging risks and changing market dynamics. The cumulative effect is that unspoken 'rules' go unchallenged, creating blind spots in strategic thinking and the ultimate risk of bypassing sound opportunities that can lead to excellent investment outcomes.

Let's look at some of the biggest myths around strategy. Understanding these will give you a better lens through which to see stronger investment opportunities. Here are the myths we will bust in this chapter:

1. *Everyone thinks you should buy an apartment, thinking you can't afford a house.*

2. *Everyone thinks you should sacrifice cashflow for capital growth, or the other way around.*

3. *Everyone thinks 'blue-chip suburbs' and 'investment-grade housing' are the best ways to invest.*

4. *Everyone thinks it's either timing the market or time in the market.*

5. *Everyone thinks you need to inspect properties.*

Busting each of these myths will include evidence through a mix of charts and graphs. It wouldn't be an InvestorKit resource without these!

ARJUN'S INSIGHT

One of the terms you'll come across is 'SA3', or by its full definition 'statistical area level 3'. This refers to a geographic area that is defined by its population spread. There are about 400 SA3 areas nationwide, and they generally comprise between 30,000 and 130,000 people.

We often refer to SA3s because the data has high statistical reliability, with a healthy number of people and transactions. People often make the mistake of only considering suburb data, searching for the 'best-growing areas' hoping to find gems, only to be led astray by remote areas up 2,000% or blue-chip areas up 597%. Beware! These lists often lack statistical reliability, with very low levels of transactions causing large fluctuations in trends and data.

1. Everyone thinks you should buy an apartment, thinking you can't afford a house.

Across many Australian major cities, median house prices are not cheap. This is especially true for Sydney, Gold Coast and parts of

Melbourne, but is evident in many other well-known locations too where the house median prices are well over $1 million. Therefore, it seems natural for investors to buy a cheaper asset type – apartments – rather than houses in popular suburbs to enter these 'premium' markets.

WHAT DOES THE DATA SHOW?

Let's look at a chart showing the median prices of houses and apartments in some popular Sydney suburbs.

3 Sydney Suburbs' House vs Apartment Median Prices
Jan 2025

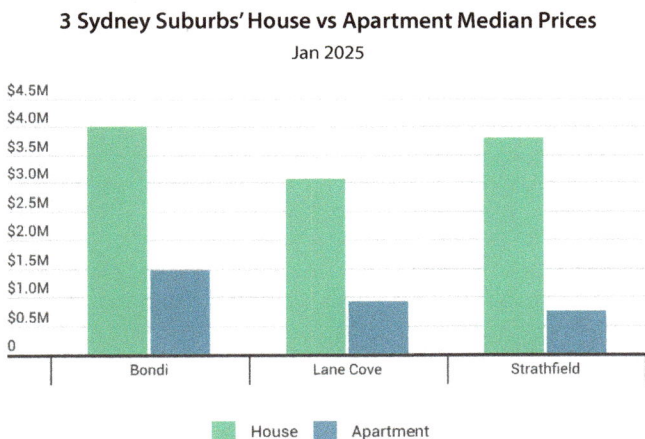

Source: Domain Insight | Prepared by InvestorKit

You can see how much cheaper the apartment markets are in these popular Sydney suburbs compared to houses in the same areas. If you bought an apartment in these suburbs, it might seem as though you've entered blue-chip markets with a lower price but it *sacrifices value growth*.

The truth is that apartments don't grow as well in value over the long term because they face the ups and downs of over-supply risks alongside poor sentiment from the many issues they face at scale. While the number of houses can be limited in many areas, the number of apartments won't be because they can expand vertically, and this impacts their growth as an investment.

To illustrate this, let's look a little deeper at the 10-year growth of the same figures.

3 Sydney Suburbs' Indexed Median Price Growth
House vs Apartment, 2014–2024 (2014 = 1.0)

Source: Domain Insight | Prepared by InvestorKit

You can see that in the 10 years from 2014 to 2024, the three house markets have all increased by over 100% in value, but their corresponding unit markets' performance was far poorer. There may be some apartments (for example, Bondi apartments) that grow better than average, but the growth is much lower compared to their house counterparts.

Is it true you can't afford a house?

No. You *can* afford a house. You're just not looking at the right locations. The five SA3 regions opposite enjoyed under $550,000 median house prices in 2014 and have all achieved over 110% total growth in the 10 years to 2024. The numbers don't lie!

5 Affordable SA3 Regions Where House Prices Grew Well in 2014–2024

Region Name	Greater Region	2014 Median House Price	2014 - 2024 Growth
Playford	Greater Adelaide	$240,600	113% (+9% p.a.)
Shoalhaven	Rest of NSW	$360,000	129% (+9% p.a.)
Mildura	Rest of Vic.	$200,000	126% (+8% p.a.)
Caboolture Hinterland	Greater Brisbane	$355,000	125% (+8% p.a.)
Buderim	Rest of Qld	$514,950	118% (+8% p.a.)

Source: Domain Insight | Prepared by InvestorKit

2. Everyone thinks you should sacrifice cashflow for capital growth, or the other way around.

Many investors believe you must choose between good capital growth and healthy cashflow. For example, if you buy in a premium suburb, you'll attract fast capital growth, but low rental income. On the other hand, if you buy in smaller or regional cities, you'll attract good rental returns but slow capital growth. Is this true?

WHAT DOES THE DATA SHOW?

Let's look at property market growth over the last decade.

2014 Rental Yield Range vs Average 10Y Growth

2014–2024

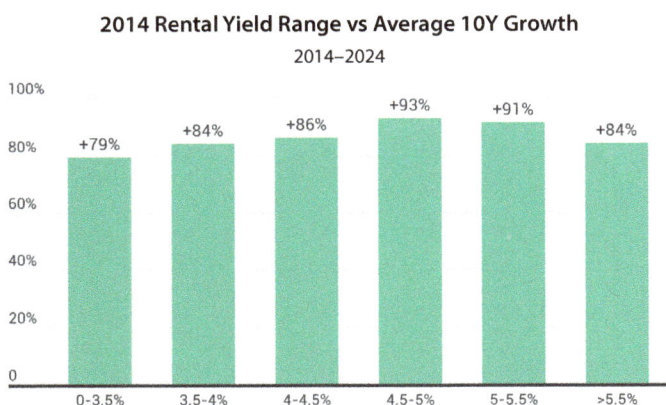

Source: Domain Insight | Prepared by InvestorKit

13

Admittedly, the regions with the lowest rental yields generally performed better during the eight years leading to 2022, as low-yield cities (especially Sydney) experienced two booms during that period. However, in 2023 and 2024, affordable cities with healthy rental yields (an initial yield of 4.5% to 5.5%) demonstrated their resilience and emerged as the ultimate winners.

A strategic investor doesn't follow any trend that only show-cases variance in the extremes (lowest yield vs highest yield). The middle sweet spot offers both healthy yield and great performance, scaling your portfolio and providing 'total return'. This also allows you to grow a portfolio and find comfort in holding the assets through cashflow.

The following two charts show this in more detail. No matter whether long term (10 years) or short term (two years), many regions achieve impressive value growth while enjoying healthy (>4%) to high yields (>5%).

Count of Long-Term Performers by 2014 Yield Range
2014–2024, Annual Growth ≥ 7%

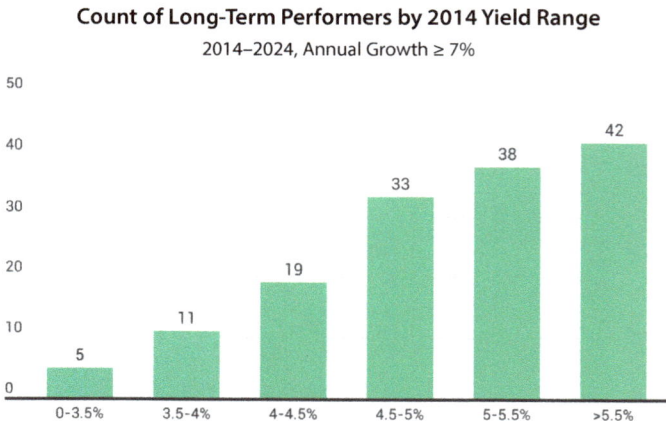

Source: Domain Insight | Prepared by InvestorKit

14

Count of Short-Term Performers by 2022 Yield Range

2022–2024, Annual Growth ≥ 10%

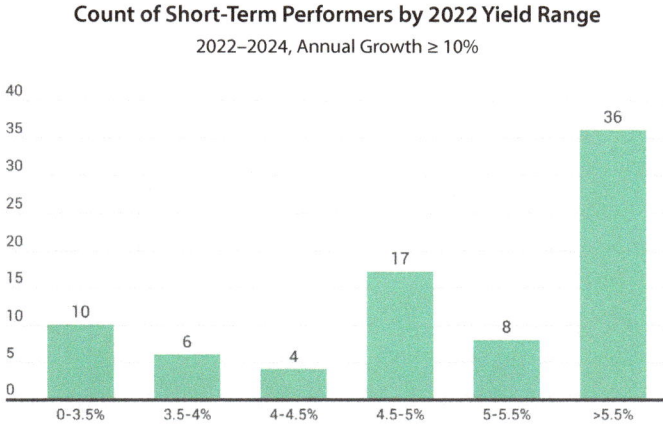

Source: Domain Insight | Prepared by InvestorKit

3. Everyone thinks 'blue-chip suburbs' and 'investment-grade housing' are the best ways to invest.

First, let's start with the phrase 'blue-chip suburbs', which starts with bias, not data. In my experience, these don't necessarily perform any better than others, yet they're consistently referred to as 'blue chips'. Many people like to assume that:

- 'Expensive suburbs must have grown a lot; cheap suburbs must have grown little.'

- 'I really want to live in that popular seaside suburb; everyone else must want to live there, too.'

- 'Regional towns don't have corporate jobs – who would want to move there?'

However, none of the above can be proven by data.

One of the most popular myths around this is that blue-chip suburbs promise constant high-value growth. But only investing in 'blue-chip suburbs' and 'investment-grade housing' are nothing but marketing phrases. These come from sales agents, investors, finance advisers – and they're all wrong, because there's no such thing as a 'blue-chip suburb'. The so-called blue-chip suburbs are no different from others.

WHAT DOES THE DATA SHOW?

Sydney's Vaucluse, Bondi and Manly are commonly considered 'blue-chip suburbs'. The following chart shows how these three suburbs' median house prices have grown over the past 10 years.

The total growth seems high. However, is the growth constant?

No. Their house values declined in 2018–19, just like every other Sydney suburb, and didn't grow much until the COVID boom in 2020–2022. As interest rates hiked in 2022 and 2023, these house values again stopped growing.

3 Blue Chip Suburbs 10Y House Price Growth
2014–2024

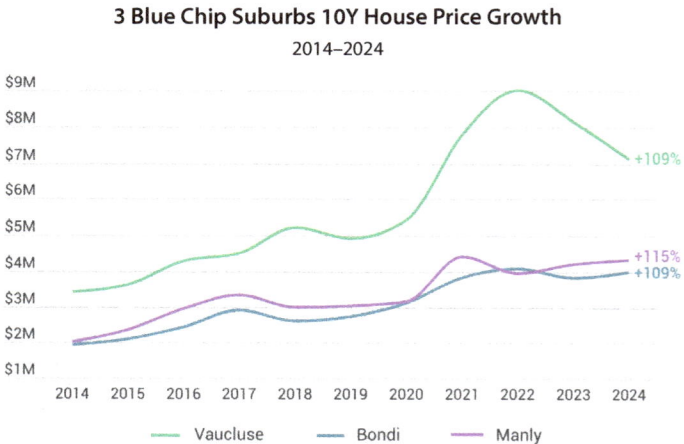

Source: Domain Insight | Prepared by InvestorKit

Now, let's look at some 'non–blue-chip suburbs'. You may not have heard of them, but their long-term growth easily beats the so-called 'blue-chip suburbs'.

3 Non-Blue-Chip Suburbs 10Y House Price Growth
2014–2024

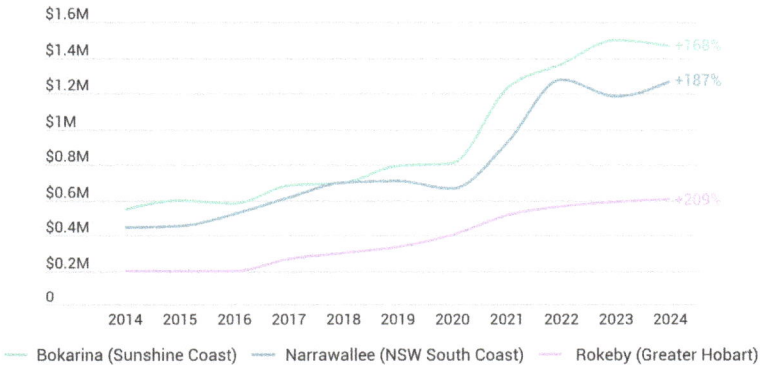

Source: Domain Insight | Prepared by InvestorKit

It's easy to see that all three non-blue-chip suburbs have out-performed the previous three suburbs over 10 years.

At the end of the day, remember two things.

Firstly, all markets are subject to market cycles, and no sub-urb is immune to natural ups and downs. Secondly, value growth is led by a combination of demand, supply, market confidence, economic activity and many other factors, not just location. An expensive location is expensive not because it's grown more but more likely because it was originally expensive. A myth!

Now, let's consider 'investment-grade property', which suggests that this is the safest type of property to buy. You may have heard this one: 'Less than 5% of properties in Australia are investment-grade.'

But if you do a quick online search for 'investment-grade property', you'll see many definitions. Unlike universally accepted terms like 'vacancy rates' or 'days on market', 'investment-grade property' is a chameleon. It changes its definition depending on who you ask. That's a clear sign it doesn't objectively exist.

In reality, 'investment-grade' is a subjective label created by individuals who want to sell you properties or strategies. It's all part of a marketing game to make things seem more sophisticated and convincing. Chasing after these elusive properties is not a wise investment strategy.

WHAT DOES THE DATA SHOW?

In the 20 years from 2004 to 2024, close to 85% of Australian SA3s with valid property market data have seen 5%+ compound annual growth in house prices. Close to one-third of them have surged by 6% per year or more.

What this shows is most of the SA3s have experienced healthy annual growth, and they're not limited to specific states or regions – they're Australia-wide. With so many SA3s achieving remarkable growth (85%), can you still believe that only less than 5% of properties qualify as 'investment-grade'?

Consider different markets that offer inland versus seaside properties. Manly and Bondi beaches in Sydney are among the most famous beaches in the world. How do their local SA3s' house price growth compare with inland SA3s'?

The following chart shows the house price trends in four Sydney SA3s: Manly and Eastern Suburbs – North are seaside featuring famous beaches, while Baulkham Hills and Ku-ring-gai are inland.

Again, the data shows that growth is consistent regardless of whether the property is seaside or inland. And while the property prices in the Manly and North and Eastern Suburbs are some of the highest in Sydney, the house value growth rates are on par with other markets inland in the same city during the same time period.

10Y House Price Trend of 4 Sydney SA3s
2014–2024

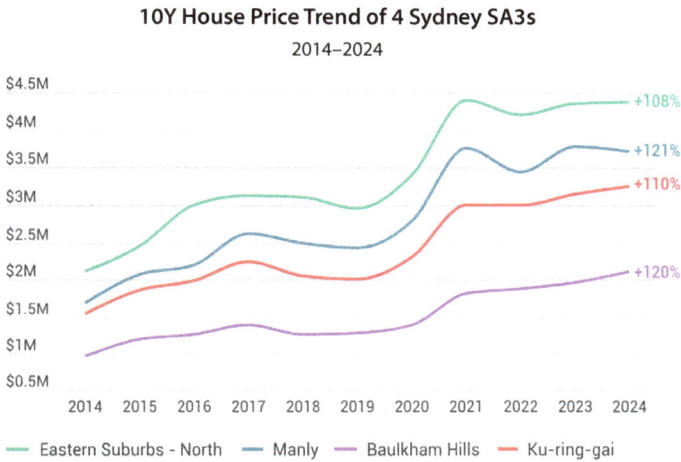

+108%
+121%
+110%
+120%

Eastern Suburbs - North — Manly — Baulkham Hills — Ku-ring-gai

Source: Domain Insight | Prepared by InvestorKit

4. Everyone thinks it's either timing the market or time in the market.

We all know that time in the market is more important than timing the market. Generally, the longer you hold your portfolio, the better growth you achieve. However, tightening your acquisition window doesn't mean sacrificing short-term growth. It's possible to time the market while maximising your time in the market.

To identify high-pressure markets that will help you to ensure healthy short-term growth, consider the following indicators (we will go through both of these in detail in the next part):

- inventory
- rental vacancy rate.

There are many more, but these two are strong indicators that you can achieve short-term growth for prices and rents.

WHAT DOES THE DATA SHOW?

Let's take SA3 regions as an example. Australia has in total 358 SA3 regions, among which 330 have consistent property market data for the past 10 years. The following chart shows the number of SA3s achieving double-digit growth each year in the decade (for 2021 and 2022, I've lifted the growth rate criteria from 10%+ to 20%+ as very few regions didn't achieve 10%+ growth during the COVID property boom).

In the last decade, we can typically see over 50 regions performing exceptionally well each year (with 10% or more annual growth). Even in 2018 and 2019, which are believed to be the Australian property market's downturn period, we still find close to 20 regions that grew well each year. This shows that every single year there are markets that enjoy very strong rates of capital growth. While long-term holding for growth is key, a priority should always be to time the market with each acquisition to align with what your portfolio needs.

Count of SA3s with Double-Digit Growth Each Year
2015–2024

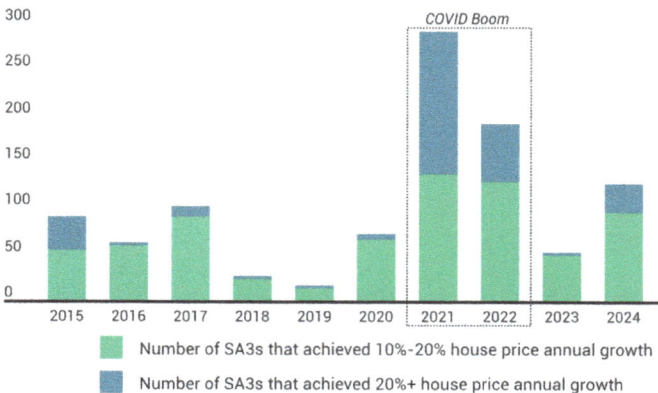

Number of SA3s that achieved 10%-20% house price annual growth

Number of SA3s that achieved 20%+ house price annual growth

Source: Domain Insight | Prepared by InvestorKit

5. Everyone thinks you need to inspect properties.

As I mentioned briefly in my introduction, I've bought every single investment property for my portfolio without stepping a foot inside it. Sight unseen. In fact, the only house I've bought after seeing it in real life is the one I live in.

As a nation obsessed with property, it might seem crazy to have only personally inspected one home across my portfolio, but the truth is that across the country when you're buying properties in capital cities, regional or rural areas – you don't need to see them to buy them.

Typically, there are two main objections when buying property unseen:

- Don't you want to see it when you're putting so much money into the investment?

- What do you do if something happens to the house and you're far away?

Firstly, a clue to the answer is in the first question. When it comes to investing, I'm not buying for emotional reasons. If the data stacks up, that's enough of a reason for me to move forward. Conversely, if you go all the way in with deep research, flights, hotels, speaking with locals, time and emotion – how likely are you then to say no if the red flags are up? You're more likely to look past the red flags to avoid going through all that again elsewhere. You can't be everywhere at once.

You still need to put in the effort for your due diligence (you'll read about this in part IV). When purchasing a home to live in, it's essential to see it in person; however, for an investment property, you don't need to.

This leads to the second objection.

If something goes wrong, I've got faith in the specialists who will manage the property on my behalf. I realise that I'm no better at rental compliance and local rental demand analysis than the property manager in that area. I'm no better at understanding the structure of the building than a pest and building inspector, and my two eyes and conversations with locals are no better than what the data says. Leave all this to the professionals!

Given so much time and money is spent on market and property research, due diligence, inspections and understanding what's required to buy in different states, it's unlikely you would buy a property outside your region because of the effort involved.

But that's a mistake, because only buying in your backyard, suburb or city can lead to a huge opportunity cost over the long term. By not selecting an area that will grow well, you could limit your equity access and ability to scale your portfolio for the future. Unfortunately, many people fall into this trap because buying locally feels safe, comfortable and easier to manage.

Having a hybrid approach at scale with a national team around you is how you truly get ahead. Furthermore, using data to locate the highest-growth areas for your budget in line with your portfolio plan will also help you progress. Use data-driven due diligence to rule out properties that don't pass all the checks and have on-the-ground contacts for videos, the truth and checks instead.

Let's look at a Sydney example.

WHAT DOES THE DATA SHOW?

Let's say you live in Sydney's Inner West and were looking to buy an investment property at the end of 2017 valued at $500,000 to $800,000. The following chart shows the number of SA3s you could choose from in each region level.

As you can see, if you were only looking in the Inner West, you would find no house in that price range. This is because the Inner West SA3 median house prices were all well above $1.5 million. But, if you expanded your search area, there were up to 98 regions available Australia-wide.

Count of SA3s with Median House Price of $500K–$800K in 2017

Source: Domain Insight | Prepared by InvestorKit

Taking this a step further, you can see in the next charts that investing within your budget outside your backyard yields a better return once you see the median growth rate five years on. So not only could you keep within your budget, but you could triple your growth – if you had invested in regional Queensland with 60+%.

SA3s Within Your Backyard

SA3s within your Backyard	Broader Region	Median Price 2017	Median Price 2022	5-Year Growth %
Canada Bay	Sydney Inner West	$2,015,000	$2,625,000	+30.3%
Leichhardt	Sydney Inner West	$1,720,000	$2,100,000	+22.1%
Strathfield - Burwood - Ashfield	Sydney Inner West	$1,725,000	$1,950,000	+13.0%

Source: Domain Insight | Prepared by InvestorKit

SA3s Within Your Budget

SA3s within your Budget	Broader Region	Median Price 2017	Median Price 2022	5-Year Growth %
Bringelly - Green Valley	Metro Sydney	$760,000	$1,030,000	+35.5%
Wyong	Greater Sydney	$570,000	$835,000	+46.5%
Queanbeyan	Regional NSW	$560,000	$895,000	+59.8%
Prospect - Walkerville	Greater Adelaide	$722,000	$1,100,000	+52.4%
Chermside	Greater Brisbane	$610,000	$976,250	+60.0%
Buderim	Regional QLD	$605,000	$1,001,000	+65.5%

Source: Domain Insight | Prepared by InvestorKit

Once you realise the power of investing beyond your backyard, you'll start to understand how it's possible to accelerate your portfolio and stop listening to the noise! By being open to all markets in your budget, your chances of success immediately multiply.

Unfortunately, there are many who would have seen that their backyard didn't fit their budget, put off investing for many years, complained about house prices, or would have opted to purchase an apartment not realising the mistake they were making.

Think of the opportunity cost of not acting.

Chapter 3

MYTHS ABOUT LOCATION AND TRENDS

W hen it comes to myth busting, this category contains one of the biggest myths – around positioning. Even just the three words 'location, location, location' have been made into a hit television show, and most of us will have heard this phrase throughout our lives.

It suggests that the single most important investment factor is where the property is located. While I spent some of the previous chapter explaining how I buy properties sight unseen and that location is important, it's not the be all and end all. Location – and trends – are only part of the story.

Here's what we'll cover next:

1. *Everyone thinks regional housing growth only boomed during COVID.*

2. *Everyone thinks you should chase higher income and low crime areas, and avoid older demographics.*

3. *Everyone thinks research means focusing on schools, shops, beaches and train stations.*

4. *Everyone thinks population growth is important for success in property investing.*

1. Everyone thinks regional housing growth only boomed during COVID.

Many people believe the regional property market boom was a COVID-related thing. And that regional property markets perform so poorly that it was only the 'exodus-from-big-cities' trend during COVID that could boost them.

But the data shows a different story.

Firstly, it's common knowledge that COVID and all the factors that occurred during that time, particularly the work-from-home trend, greatly influenced regional Australia's time to shine. The regional property boom was especially impressive in Queensland, South Australia and Western Australia, but most Australian cities experienced growth beyond their capital.

But they were booming before COVID as well, as you can see from the following chart showing three regional New South Wales cities and Greater Sydney's annual growth rates from 2014 to 2024.

WHAT DOES THE DATA SHOW?

You can see that Kiama – Shellharbour saw 10%+ annual growth for three years from 2014 to 2017, while Port Stephens and Orange experienced well above average growth for a consecutive few years before 2020, which are both deemed as booms considering national averages are typically between 5% and 7% p.a. long term in Australia.

Median House Price Growth Rate Trends

3 NSW Regional Cities vs Greater Sydney, 2014–2024

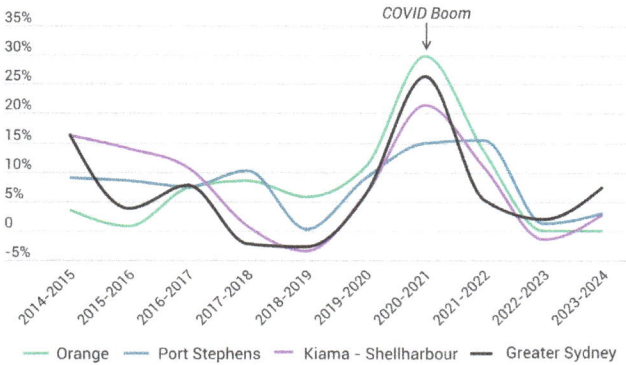

Source: Domain Insight | Prepared by InvestorKit

Now let's look at the four regions' growth before and after the start of the COVID property boom (June 2020).

4.5 Years' Total Growth Before and After June 2020

	Dec 2015 - Jun 2020	Jun 2020 - Dec 2024
Greater Sydney	*7.1%*	*52.2%*
Orange	26.9%	60.0%
Port Stephens	29.1%	51.1%
Kiama - Shellharbour	20.8%	44.1%

Source: Domain Insight | Prepared by InvestorKit

You can see that all three regional SA3s grew more than Sydney before the COVID boom.

What this highlights is that regional areas offer excellent investment opportunities, despite the myth that capital city investing is best. I believe a capital vs regional mindset is not healthy for investors and will hold success back, while an open mind will help you achieve your investment goals faster.

There are three reasons for this:

1. You get to choose an asset from a much bigger pool.

2. Capital cities don't necessarily grow more quickly.

3. You don't buy a 'capital city' when you buy in one – it's all about the local market.

Today, regional cities have so much growth potential underpinned by their strong housing demand and low supply levels. With job opportunities in regional Australia increasing faster than in capital cities, due to government infrastructure investment, this will continue to attract an enormous number of people to call the regions home.

Regional growth will also continue to be fuelled by housing affordability, one of the most significant drivers of population movement. That's why we see a growing trend of migration from expensive cities (especially Sydney) to more affordable cities which started well before the pandemic.

As long as the local market is enjoying good economic growth momentum and rising market pressure, it could be worth investing no matter where it is.

2. Everyone thinks you should chase higher income and low crime areas, and avoid older demographics.

I'm sure you've heard these before:

- 'Wealthier locations grow better.'

- 'The lower the crime rate, the better the growth.'

- 'Retirement towns are bad investment locations.'

These are good myths about location.

Let's look at average income level and residents' median age in the next two charts.

WHAT DOES THE DATA SHOW?

Australian SA3s 1Y and 10Y House Price Growth by Initial Average Personal Income Range

1Y = 2012–13, 10Y = 2012–22

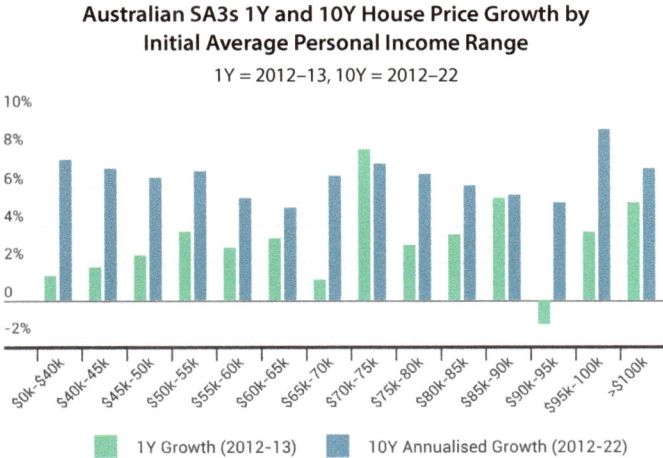

Source: ABS, Domain Insight | Prepared by InvestorKit

Australian SA3s 1Y and 10Y House Price Growth by Initial Median Resident Age

1Y = 2012–13, 10Y = 2012–22

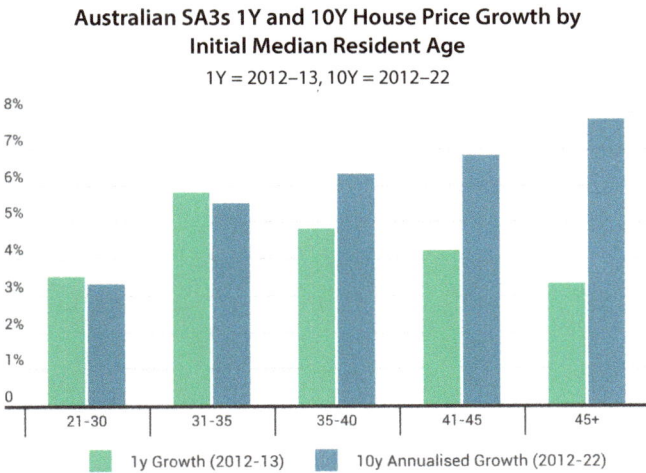

Source: ABS, Domain Insight | Prepared by InvestorKit

You can see there is no clear relationship between income level and growth rate (short term or long term). Those factors do partially affect a market's property price and growth, but

29

they're neither the sole influencer nor any more important than the others. All influences need to be examined together when analysing a market.

Many investors are concerned about crime. They assume that a higher crime rate means lower demand in the sales and rental markets, leading to lower capital and rental growth.

Now, let's look at the total number of crimes in every New South Wales suburb in 2014 and test the correlation between the crime rate (Number of crimes ÷ Population) and house price growth in one year, five years and ten years.

The data shows there is no statistically significant correlation between the 2014 crime rate and price growth in the next year and five years. The negative correlation is statistically significant in the 10-year test, but the coefficient of −0.43 is too small to be a concern. We can confidently conclude that the crime rate doesn't necessarily correlate with price growth or rental growth, as price growth displays the same trends.

It might, however, affect your cashflow in the form of higher maintenance costs if you have bad tenants, or higher insurance premiums owing to a higher-crime-rate area. However, these areas tend to have higher rental yields, which can mitigate the impact.

NSW Suburbs' 2014 Crime Rates vs 1Y-5Y-10Y House Price Growth

1Y = 2014–15, 5Y = 2014–19, 10Y = 2014–24

Crime Rate vs. 1Y Growth:

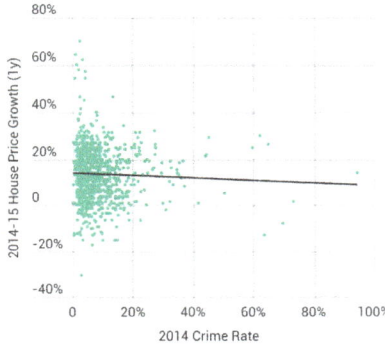

Crime Rate vs. 5Y Growth:

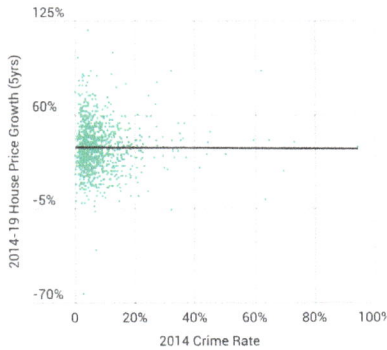

Crime Rate vs. 10Y Growth:

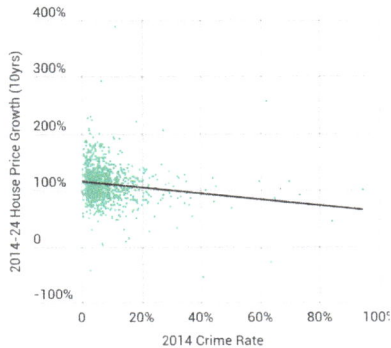

Source: ABS; Domain Insight; NSW Government | Prepared by InvestorKit

3. Everyone thinks research means focusing on schools, shops, beaches and train stations.

Some investors believe that properties around top schools, shopping centres, beaches or train stations grow faster in value and generate higher rental income. I can see the connection because amenities such as public transport, good schools, shopping centres, beaches or distance to the CBD are important when people decide on a place to live.

However, as an investor, these factors are not as essential.

WHAT DOES THE DATA SHOW?

Let's look at two suburbs in Melbourne: Berwick and Endeavour Hills, within the LGA of Casey.

Berwick and Endeavour Hills Median House Price Trends
2012–2022

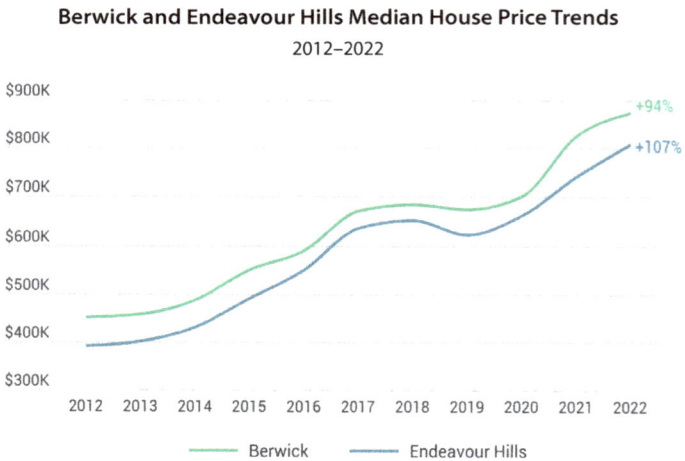

Source: ABS, Domain Insight | Prepared by InvestorKit

Berwick is close to the selective school Nossal High School, which is ranked No. 17 in Victoria, while Endeavour Hills is in the catchment of the public school Gleneagles Secondary College, which is ranked below 300 in Victoria.

If top schools equal higher value growth and higher rental income, Berwick must have been performing much better than Endeavour Hills. However, the data doesn't show that.

The opposite holds true: Endeavour Hills has outperformed Berwick. The truth is that the schools' impact on the surrounding suburbs is more reflected by house prices and rental price levels instead of growth rates. You may need to pay more for a Berwick house and be able to sell it for a higher-than-average price because of the top school, but the growth rates in between are in line with the broader market.

Data shows that the 'popular' amenities and close proximity to CBD may make their surrounding areas more expensive but not grow faster as price variance has already factored in their appeal. What's more, an area without such amenities may have other attractive features, and they could be different from your preferences.

You may like the parks, someone else may like the shops, you may like peace and quiet and someone else may love the hustle of a busy community. You may like broad diversity; others may enjoy being surrounded by a quiet community and that speaks their language.

The data proves that these factors don't significantly impact value growth rates. And while prices may vary based on proximity to amenities, growth rates remain largely unaffected. 'Each to their own' is the saying, so rather than assuming what amenities or things are better, I let the growth data do the talking and not just the price.

4. Everyone thinks population growth is important for success in property investing.

Economists love praising population growth and the media often quotes statistics around these numbers. Naturally, many novice property investors think that buying in an area with a fast-growing population is a good idea, as population growth means increasing housing demand and a livelier economy and community. The conclusion is there will be good capital growth and rental income.

But there are two key questions to consider:

1. Why does the population grow?

2. Does the population growth indicate higher demand or higher supply?

Firstly, population grows due to natural growth (more births than deaths) and migration (more people moving in than out). When it comes to migration, let's look a little closer at one of the top destinations for migrants in Australia: Auburn, in Western Sydney.

WHAT DOES THE DATA SHOW?

As you can see in the chart, Auburn's annual population growth rate has always been higher than Greater Sydney's average, except in 2020–21 when Australia's international border was closed.

Auburn vs Greater Sydney Population Growth Rate Trends
2012–2023

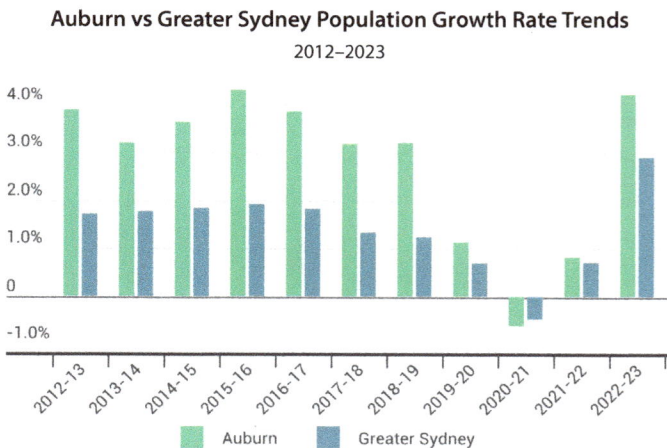

Source: ABS | Prepared by InvestorKit

Then, if we look at how the housing market had been growing over the same period:

Auburn Median House Price, Sales Volume vs Population Growth Rate Trends

2013–2023

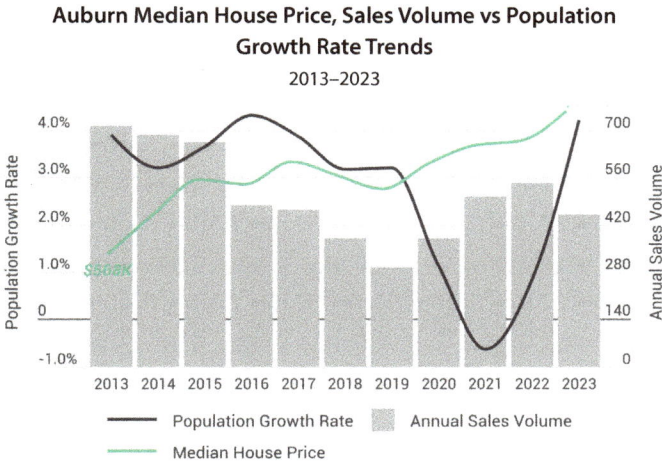

Source: ABS, Domain Insight | Prepared by InvestorKit

Here, you can see that sales volumes, which usually indicate housing demand, didn't move in line with the population growth. On the contrary, there was a rise from 2019 onwards, when the population was falling.

On the other hand, median house prices grew by 92.1% over the 10 years, lower than the Greater Sydney average of 101.6%, despite the stronger population growth.

As with natural growth, population growth caused by immigrants does not necessarily bring better growth in a localised area.

Population growth can also be considered a supply response metric. For example, if a large level of population growth occurs in a new outer ring suburb, in most cases it means that the housing availability is there to house them. Therefore, this doesn't mean demand is outpacing supply, this is supply responding to demand

and now more people are housed in an area. Population growth isn't the main driver, population pressure is. Pressure is the number of people able and willing to purchase in an area being substantially higher than the quantity of homes available online for sale and in the pipeline built without sufficient supply in surrounding areas too.

Furthermore, population pressure can be caused by shifts in the same population better than it can from a new wave of international migrants. For example, a divorce or adult-aged kids moving out of home are going to create more households required for the same number of total people, which impacts housing demand as a result.

Another myth busted!

Chapter 4

MYTHS ABOUT THE PROPERTY

Given we've tackled myths about strategy and location, it's time to zero in on the false assumptions around the properties themselves. Again, there are plenty. Apartments versus houses? Greater land size equals greater growth? How many bedrooms and bathrooms? All of these assumptions are fed to us from the moment we begin researching and start looking for that first property.

It's important to define what's based on data and what ends up being circulated as truth but couldn't be further from it.

Here's what we'll cover in this chapter:

1. *Everyone thinks that the number of beds, baths, building materials and age matters.*

2. *Everyone thinks that buying 'off-the-plan' offers better purchasing prices.*

3. *Everyone thinks the bigger land, the better the growth.*

4. *Everyone thinks being close to train stations (and other amenities) is important.*

1. Everyone thinks that the number of beds, baths, building materials and age matters.

As we've discovered, many factors contribute to achieving better growth. When it comes to bricks and mortar, the popular story is that the number of rooms, the building materials or the age of the house matters to value growth.

Here's some food for thought. Would you pay:

- An extra $200,000 for a four-bedroom rather than a three-bedroom house?

- An extra $50,000 for one more bathroom?

- An extra $150,000 for a brick house instead of a weatherboard house?

Let's look at two real-life case studies.

WHAT DOES THE DATA SHOW?

Consider two houses with a different number of bedrooms located close to each other in the Brisbane suburb of Sherwood. They were sold around the same time in 2018 and again in 2022. The chart shows their details.

Number of Rooms Case Study

Address	Bed-Bath-Car	2018 Sale Price	2022 Sale Price	Growth Rate
9 Cormack Street Sherwood QLD 4075	3x 2x 2x	$1,130,000	$1,675,000	48%
19 Weinholt Street Sherwood QLD 4075	4x 2x 2x	$1,355,000	$1,955,000	44%

Source: RP Data | Prepared by InvestorKit

You'll notice they grew similarly percentage-wise, in a similar suburb and with similar prices at a similar time, even though one property had another bedroom. The key here is that the extra bedroom doesn't change 'price growth percentage'. It only changes the 'price paid' to purchase it.

If your budget gets you into a suburb but it's a three-bedroom property and you can't afford the four-bedroom property, the percentage growth won't be widely affected, as evidenced here over the long term. The price variance is already set.

The Weinholt St value increased by $600,000, seemingly higher than Property A ($545,000), where its growth rate is slightly lower due to the higher initial price. This highlights that even though the Weinholt St property had the extra bedroom, it didn't record any higher percentage growth in the same market transacting at the same time.

WHAT DOES THE DATA SHOW?

Consider two houses with different external wall materials. They are close to each other in the Brisbane suburb of Corinda. They were sold around the same time in 2014 and again in 2022. The chart shows their details.

External Wall Materials Case Study

Address	Bed-Bath-Car	External Wall	2014 Sale Price	2022 Sale Price	Growth Rate
312 Cliveden Avenue Corinda QLD 4075	3x 2x 2x	Brick	$760,000	$1,215,000	60%
7 Rathlyn Avenue Corinda QLD 4075	4x 2x 2x	Weatherboard	$1,060,000	$1,754,000	65%

Source: RP Data | Prepared by InvestorKit

While the Rathlyn St property has weatherboard external walls, which is believed to be 'worse' than brick, it grew similarly to the brick house in Cliveden Ave. It's also noted that it's a four-bedroom property; however, we proved that this doesn't matter in the previous example.

Both examples by no means suggest that smaller houses outperform bigger ones, or that weatherboard is better than brick. What they show is that house growth rates are not affected by the number of rooms (or the number of bedrooms, bathrooms, and so on), materials or age.

Growth is determined by the demand and supply of the local market.

ARJUN'S INSIGHT

Focus on the market, not the property. When buying, comparable sales will be key.

Don't fall in love with the property or become overly focused on aesthetic checklists. The market and cycle timing will do the heavy lifting after you conduct due diligence and pay the right price based on comparable sales analysis.

2. Everyone thinks that buying 'off-the-plan' offers better purchasing prices.

As Australia's housing affordability worsens in many areas, off-the-plan properties are a popular option for homebuyers and investors, especially in major cities. One of the key selling points is a 'better' purchasing price, either through early-bird promotions or because of 'buying at the current value, settling at the future value'.

But there are three reasons why buying off-the-plan is not a good idea:

- valuation shortfalls
- delays in construction
- uncertainty in demographics data.

Valuation shortfalls

When buying off-the-plan, you're not paying for the property's current value. You're paying for the developer and builder's margins, sales agents' commissions, marketing campaigns, premiums for future market value, incentive costs and more. That's fine if the market continues to grow as the developer expects during construction.

However, markets don't always grow. In a declining market, you may face valuation shortfalls, which could cause trouble. *If you don't have enough cash to make up for a valuation shortfall, you could end up letting go of the deal and lose your deposit. A purchase that was supposed to save money could turn out to be a costly mistake.*

Delays in construction

Issues with the build can occur at any time due to weather, shortage of construction materials, shipment issues, authority approvals and other unforeseen circumstances. During COVID, many developers and builders faced huge delays, which all fed into their bottom line. You can see this in the following table, which shows the average number of months to complete a development project for three property types – houses, townhouses and apartments – from 2015 to 2023.

WHAT DOES THE DATA SHOW?

Average Number of Months to Build a Dwelling Unit

	2015-16	2020-21	2022-23
House	-	8.7	11.7
Townhouse	-	12.7	14.9
Apartment Building	21	30.6	28.8

Source: Kanebrigde News | Prepared by InvestorKit

The construction time increased by 34% for houses and 17% for townhouses from 2020 to 2023. The reasons behind the delays include the global supply chain disruption and other local conditions during the COVID years. The figure for apartment constructions decreased slightly, but was still much higher than the 2015–16 level.

All delays mean spending more money. This might be extending your current lease if it's your first residence or being prepared for a longer vacancy period and a lower rental price if settlement is delayed and many others are finishing at a similar time.

Uncertainty in demographics data

Demographics are not determining factors of price growth, but their impact can still play a part, especially for new areas with fast-changing data due to how new the area is.

When a region is established, the demographics are constant. You know where you're buying, who your potential tenants are and their preferences. Trends are usually established rather than forming, and this adds confidence when investing.

But when a region is new, its demographics are still developing. There is less confidence about the community, the tenant market and their preferences, and how many rental properties you'll be competing with.

WHAT DOES THE DATA SHOW?

Established suburbs demonstrate better short- to medium-term growth than new regions because their housing supply is more controllable.

Let's consider Jimboomba vs The Hills District, in Greater Brisbane. In this pair, Jimboomba is the new region. For starters, look at how high its building approval rate is compared to The Hills District.

In the five years from 2018 to 2023, The Hills District enjoyed solid growth of 53%, while Jimboomba grew by 39%.

5Y Building Approval % and Median House Price Trends
Jimboomba vs The Hills District, 2018–2023

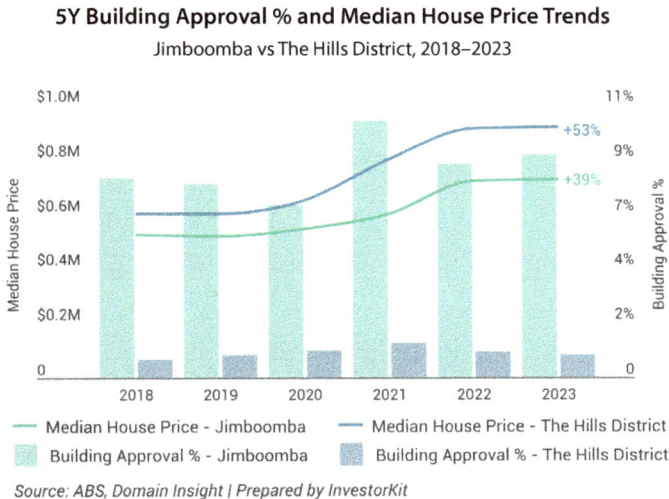

Source: ABS, Domain Insight | Prepared by InvestorKit

Looking back at the three pitfalls I've outlined, they have one thing in common: they're all uncontrollable. And when there are too many uncontrollable factors, there's less certainty in performance. Building approval percentages in isolation aren't the core growth or declining factor; however, continuing to add more uncontrollable factors on the journey won't assist a data-driven investing decision, especially if other established housing supply and demand metrics for that newer area are weak, too. It's the trifecta of high building approvals, high vacancy rates and a large level of established listings for sale online that impact prices negatively.

3. Everyone thinks the bigger the land, the better the growth.

When it comes to property investing, the myth is that larger land grows better than smaller land.

WHAT DOES THE DATA SHOW?

Let's take a new investor, Oliver, as an example. He's excited about his first real estate investment and finds two properties in the Melbourne suburb of Seaford, by the bay. One house is on Bayside Grove, with a land size of 567 sqm, and the other is on a spacious 817 sqm block on Kananook Avenue.

Oliver is drawn to the larger plot; he believes the myth that more land leads to better growth. But after looking through the properties' sales histories, he discovers a different story:

2 Melbourne Houses' Land Size and 9Y Growth

Address	Number of Bath-Bath-Car	Land Size (m²)	2014 Sold Price	2023 Sold Price	9-Year Growth
35 Bayside Grove, Seaford, VIC 3198	3-1-3	567	$419,000	$750,000	+79.0%
52 Kananook Avenue, Seaford, VIC 3198	3-1-6	817	$515,000	$918,000	+78.3%

Source: RP Data | Prepared by InvestorKit

Not everyone prefers more land. Large plots come with higher maintenance costs, requiring significant upkeep, whether landscaping, fencing or general property management, leading to substantial ongoing expenses.

For investors, large land size also means a higher purchase price and a lower yield (as large land doesn't increase rental price much). Furthermore, bigger plots are potentially more sensitive to market fluctuations as demand for them is more volatile.

You may notice a key theme occurring among these trends, which is many people assume that the price of an asset is a growth advantage. But growth rates aren't as impressive as many think.

The above example covers land size within the same suburb and the timing of the purchase and sale. In more extreme examples, we can question why hectares of land in Broken Hill, for example, are cheaper than smaller land parcels in other regional centres. Not all land is equal when locations vary, and land size alone won't increase growth rates in the same suburb if you end up paying much more for that land.

4. Everyone thinks being close to train stations (and other amenities) is important.

Do these sound familiar?

- 'You should buy something near a train station.'
- 'Why don't you buy a house near that new shopping centre? Great potential!'
- 'This beachside suburb has always been performing better than the surrounding suburbs.'
- 'The closer to the CBD, the more potential tenants you'll get.'

Amenities such as public transport, good schools, shopping centres, beaches or distance to the CBD are important for many when they decide on a place to live. But local amenities or distance to the CBD are not as important as you think to create property growth.

Let's have a look at some suburbs across the country, especially the most popular housing markets of Sydney, Melbourne and Brisbane. We are going to compare, within the same region, different suburbs with and without some of the commonly believed important features, including a train station, proximity to a top school and being close to the CBD.

First, let's look at train stations in Sydney.

WHAT DOES THE DATA SHOW?

In the SA3 of Blacktown – North, the suburbs of Quakers Hill, Schofields, Riverstone, Rouse Hill and The Ponds have one or more train/metro stations close by serving local residents, while the other suburbs – Acacia Gardens, Glenwood, Parklea and Stanhope Gardens – do not. This chart shows the median sale price of houses in these two groups from 2012 to 2021.

Blacktown – North Suburbs Median House Price Trends
with/without a train station, 2012–2021

Source: Domain Insight | Prepared by InvestorKit

The house price growth pace of suburbs with or without a train station tends to be similar, indicating that having a train station within walking distance to your property does not make your property grow faster than others.

Plus, you might think that the house value near a train station would be higher than those far from the station. But the average median house price of suburbs with train stations is lower than the opposite group, largely due to denser housing options. Myth busted!

While a train station adds value to an area from a lifestyle perspective, it can also change the local zoning and building restrictions. Building density may be higher around the train station than in the surrounding areas, leading to smaller land lots and higher-density dwellings such as townhouses or even apartment buildings. Therefore, the average property value would be lower.

Let's look at schools in Sydney – another myth.

WHAT DOES THE DATA SHOW?

In this chart, you will see that the median house price around a NSW top school is lower than neighbouring suburbs. James Ruse Agricultural High School has been ranked No. 1 in NSW for years. It's a selective school and doesn't have a catchment zone, so let's assume the suburbs within a 2 km radius are the most popular areas to live in if you attend the school and want a shorter commute. The suburbs are Epping, Oatlands, Telopea, Dundas Valley and Carlingford.

Sydney Suburbs Median House Price Trends
with/without a top school, 2012–2021

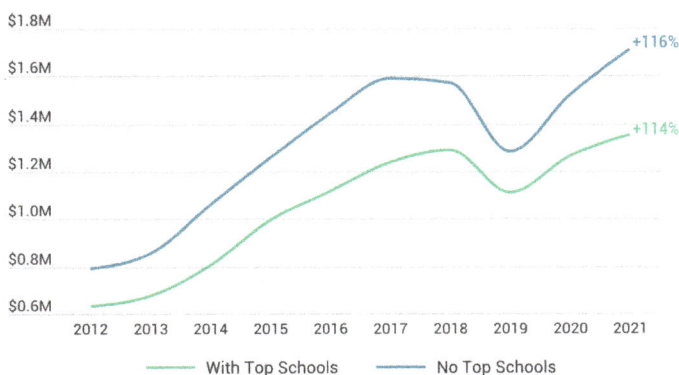

Source: Domain Insight | Prepared by InvestorKit

In comparison, Marsden High School is an average school ranked below 200 in the state, and its catchment falls in Ermington, West Ryde, Denistone East, Denistone and Eastwood, which are next to, but not overlapping, the top school's 2 km radius.

The chart shows the house price growth in the two suburb groups. The growth pace is almost the same, despite the value difference.

Properties in proximity to stations and schools, as evidenced above, do not have improved growth. The same is evident for shops, beaches and the distance to CBD. All are not as important as you may think. The data shows that these features do not make a significant difference in the growth of a given area, as they have been factored into the purchase price.

Chapter 5

MYTHS ABOUT TOOLS AND INDICATORS

You only need to visit Bunnings to realise how much Australians love their tools. When it comes to tools that apply to property, it's a similar story, and the market is full of them online and all offering benefits that sound great. Who wouldn't want a valuation that saves time and money? Who wouldn't want finance approved quickly?

The problem is that the online tools and indicators lack nuance. They offer a cookie-cutter approach that doesn't consider important details that can significantly impact what you're trying to achieve. I always advocate for taking the time to do things properly, strategically and with the right due diligence. Anything less than that and you're risking your portfolio and opportunity to put yourself in the best investment position.

Here are the myths we'll bust in this chapter:

1. *Everyone thinks that E-valuation (electronic or online valuation estimates) platforms are reliable.*

2. *Everyone thinks that due diligence isn't necessary.*

3. *Rental yield is all that matters.*

4. *You can rely on single indicators to make property decisions.*

1. Everyone thinks that E-valuation (electronic or online valuation estimates) platforms are reliable.

Some investors have a subscription to CoreLogic or other platforms that provide E-valuation reports, and they think that's good enough for them to evaluate the market. Others even sadly rely on their mortgage broker to simply print out an E-val and use that.

But is an E-valuation always reliable? No. Relying on these is one of the bigger – and easiest – mistakes investors make, leading to missing out on properties because valuations haven't caught up or are incorrect.

Here are some conditions when E-valuation or desktop valuations are considered helpful and when they are unreliable:

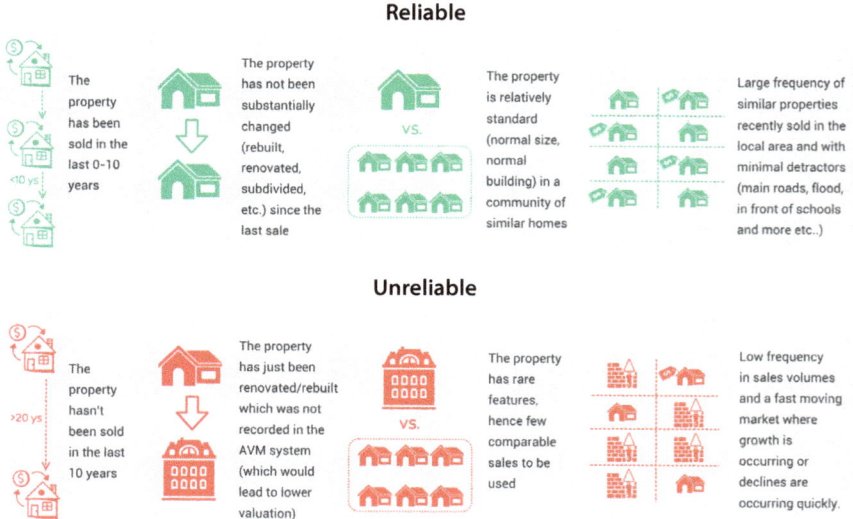

Reliable

The property has been sold in the last 0-10 years

The property has not been substantially changed (rebuilt, renovated, subdivided, etc.) since the last sale

The property is relatively standard (normal size, normal building) in a community of similar homes

Large frequency of similar properties recently sold in the local area and with minimal detractors (main roads, flood, in front of schools and more etc..)

Unreliable

The property hasn't been sold in the last 10 years

The property has just been renovated/rebuilt which was not recorded in the AVM system (which would lead to lower valuation)

The property has rare features, hence few comparable sales to be used

Low frequency in sales volumes and a fast moving market where growth is occurring or declines are occurring quickly.

When it comes to technology, online valuation platforms and automated valuation models (AVMs) are becoming smarter and smarter, emerging as the go-to tools for fast property value estimates. While they do offer speed and efficiency, cost-effectiveness and accessibility, they fall short in a few areas:

- They have limited data inputs.

- They lack human judgment and include no physical inspection.

- The accuracy can vary.

Let's consider each of these individually.

Limited data inputs

Even smart online valuation platforms have a blind spot. They rely on publicly available data, missing out on recent improvements that can sway a property's value.

WHAT DOES THE DATA SHOW?

You purchased a property for $500,000 and renovated the whole house in the six months following settlement – new kitchen, new bathrooms, new floorboards, the works. After the renovation, you wanted an updated property value. The online valuation platforms might tell you that the house is worth $525,000 because the market grew by 5% over the past year. However, an on-site valuation might show that the property is worth $650,000 considering the added value from the renovation.

Lack of human judgment and no physical inspection

Machines lack the human touch. Online valuation platforms lack the expertise and subjective judgment that human appraisers bring to the table. Consequently, they may overlook critical issues that can only be identified through a physical inspection, such as structural problems or hidden defects. Overstated valuations can give property owners a false sense of confidence.

WHAT DOES THE DATA SHOW?

Let's assume a mansion close to Sydney Harbour was divided into four apartments with the same number of bedrooms, bathrooms and similar floor area. Online valuation platforms might provide similar value estimates for each of these apartments, adjusting slightly for their levels and orientation. However, a human valuer could advise that the top-floor unit facing the Harbour Bridge and the Opera House is worth $1 million more than the others because of its stunning view.

Accuracy variability

While these platforms aim for bullseye accuracy, there's a catch. It all depends on the data quality, the algorithm's smarts and market conditions. In turbulent times, these virtual valuations might not hit the mark.

WHAT DOES THE DATA SHOW?

During a real estate market downturn, an online valuation platform may not be able to factor in the decline in property values accurately and provide overly optimistic valuation results. Trusting these results, sellers could miss out on good offers because of unrealistically high price expectations, and buyers could pay more than they should.

While online valuation platforms are fast and easy, it's essential to recognise their limitations and supplement them with human expertise. After all, automated valuations rely on online data, where the quality, quantity and timeliness of inputs are not controllable, and therefore can make a massive difference.

2. Everyone thinks that due diligence isn't necessary.

If you think you can buy any house in a hot suburb and just sit back waiting for value growth, you're wrong. Houses can appreciate differently and produce varying cashflows, even on the same street. That's why you need thorough due diligence before buying.

But due diligence isn't just property checks. It's much more than that. (You can read more about this in part IV).

Due diligence includes:

- financial due diligence

- market due diligence

- property due diligence.

Financial due diligence

Financial due diligence is not only figuring out how much you can borrow, but more importantly, setting standards for your purchase, such as price range, yield level, expected annual value and rental growth, and buffers for risk management.

For example, in early 2022, if you had factored in the potential interest hikes during your financial due diligence, you would have chosen to buy in a market with a healthy rental yield and high rental market pressure. This way, you would enjoy a rental income that covered most of your mortgage repayment (not all of it) even when interest rates rose.

Market due diligence

Market due diligence is the market research process in your purchase journey.

Here's an example: if you were to buy a property in 2016, would you buy in Sydney or Brisbane?

Although Sydney was growing robustly in 2016, market due diligence would tell you that its growth cycle was close to the peak, while the Brisbane market was showing signs of recovery after a few slow-growing years.

The two cities' performance afterwards would prove the value of your market due diligence. Although Brisbane would have still been a little on the early side by a few years, it would have been a better start than the peaks and declines that occurred in Sydney.

Indexed House Value Growth: Sydney vs Brisbane
2016–2024, Sep 2016 = 1.0

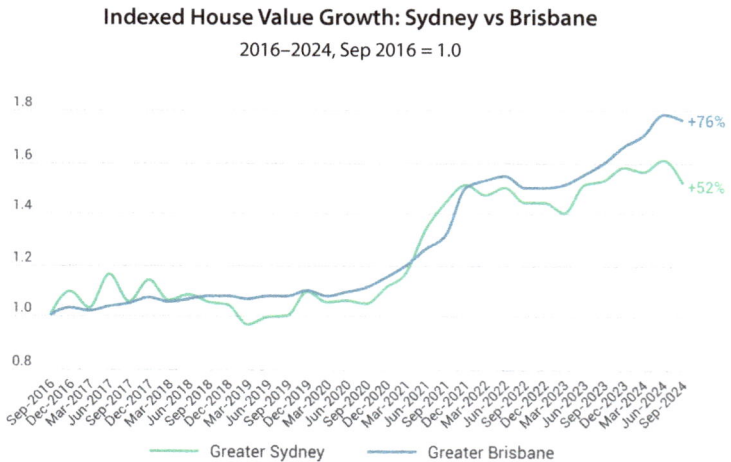

Source: ABS | Prepared by InvestorKit

Property due diligence

Even in the same suburb, different properties can experience various capital growth rates and popularity among renters, for different reasons. For example:

- A house could be impacted by major floods or a bushfire.

- A piece of land might be too small.

- A house might be too close to noisy train tracks.

- A six-bed mansion in a three- or four-bed–dominant suburb might take more time to find tenants.

Due diligence is non-negotiable. Again, there's more on this in part IV.

3. Rental yield is all that matters.

Many investors believe the higher the yield the better, because it means more rental income into your pocket. Yes, healthy rental yields are great, but putting too much attention on this can be a mistake.

What is rental yield? Rental yield is the ratio of the total rental income you receive over a year to the market value of a property.

$$\text{Rental Yield} = \frac{\text{Annual Rental Income}}{\text{Market Value}}$$

There are two types of rental yields: gross rental yield and net rental yield. The above definition is for gross rental yield, while the net figure excludes your annual expenses (insurance, maintenance, property management fees, and so on).

$$\text{Net Rental Yield} = \frac{\text{Annual Rental Income} - \text{Total Expenses}}{\text{Market Value}}$$

This equation helps determine if the investment is financially feasible and sustainable in terms of portfolio building.

Let's do a quick calculation to get a better picture of how the rental yield influences your cashflow.

WHAT DOES THE DATA SHOW?

Let's say you're going to buy a $500,000 house with:

- *80% LVR loan*
- *principal & interest (P&I) loan with a 4.5% interest rate (interest rates vary over time)*
- *35% of gross rental income to be spent on holding costs*
- *average two weeks vacant period per year*
- *rental price and expenses growing by 3% per year.*

What would the cashflow be like in the coming 30 years assuming there is no further rental growth if the initial rental yield is 5% (rent equals $480 per week), 4% (rent equals $385 per week) and 3% (rent equals $290 per week)?

Y1–Y30 Weekly Cashflow Projection by Initial Rental Yield

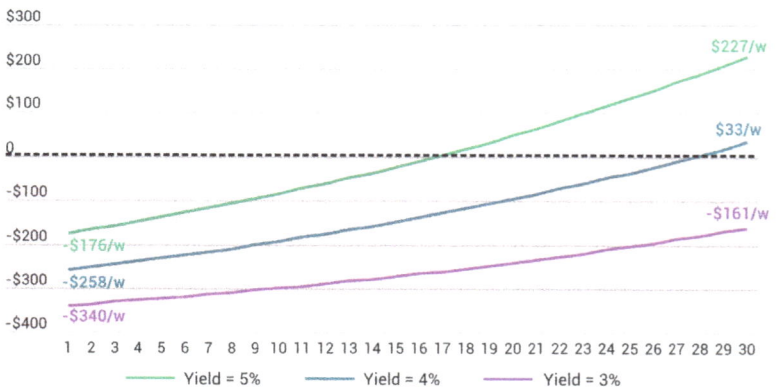

Source: InvestorKit | Prepared by InvestorKit

You can see that with a rental yield of 5%, you would need to pay $176 each week to own the property, based on a P&I loan.

However, once you've bought the house, the equation changes. Now, the house price denominator will be fixed in the yield calculation, and the change in the rental income growth becomes more important.

The equation is referred to as 'rental yield against purchase price', and changes to:

$$\text{Rental Yield} = \frac{\text{Annual Rental Income}}{\text{\st{Market Value} Purchase Price}}$$

WHAT DOES THE DATA SHOW?

Let's say you bought a $500,000 house and the initial weekly rent was $450, while the rental yield equalled 4.68%. In one year, its market value grew to $550,000, and the weekly rent grew to $500. The rental yield for someone who's going to buy it now would be around 4.73% ($500/w (52wks) ÷ $550,000 = 4.73%), but for you, the rental yield is 5.2% ($500/w (52wks) ÷ $500,000 = 5.2%).

Besides the initial rental yield, rental growth is also key to your investment success. Far too often, I've seen investors prioritise high rental yield alone and ignore rental market pressure. Their high yield locations didn't see much more rent growth, whereas the area with slightly lower rental yield (which they completely ignored) continued to grow at higher values of price growth and also grow more in rental prices. As a result, the rental yield eventually became just as high as the property they prioritised which didn't have as much rental growth, creating a flatline yield over time.

In other words, if you can handle lower rental yields, why not make your search wider across more locations? With more locations you can zone in on those with the highest rental pressure instead of fewer locations with the highest rental yields. Strong rental pressure can lift rental yields quickly for those with lower rental yields at their starting point.

4. You can rely on single indicators to make property decisions.

I've left this one until the end because it's an important one. As I covered earlier in the book, the media loves to pull out isolated indicators to report on why the market is behaving a certain way. The bigger the variance, the better the story. However, relying on one indicator only tells one part of the story. Take these popular theories:

- 'If the population is fast-growing, the property market must be booming.'

- 'If the number of sales is surging, house prices are going to surge as well.'

- 'If the national housing lending value is dropping, the housing market in every city will decline as fewer loans equals less price growth.'

While everyone likes the simple things, in property things are not simple. To create the whole picture, you need more indicators, because these combined tell the *full* story. Let's consider two examples.

WHAT DOES THE DATA SHOW?

This is a sales volume example looking at the house sales volume in Caboolture, an SA3 in Greater Brisbane. Volumes declined by 36% in three years from 2017 to 2020.

Caboolture Annual House Sales Volume Trend
2017–2020

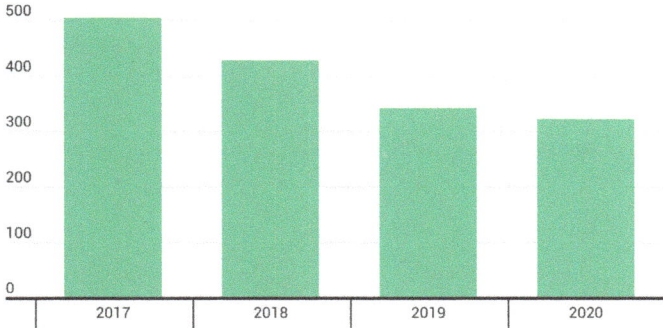

Source: Domain Insight | Prepared by InvestorKit

Caboolture Median House Price vs Sales Volume Trends
2017–2020

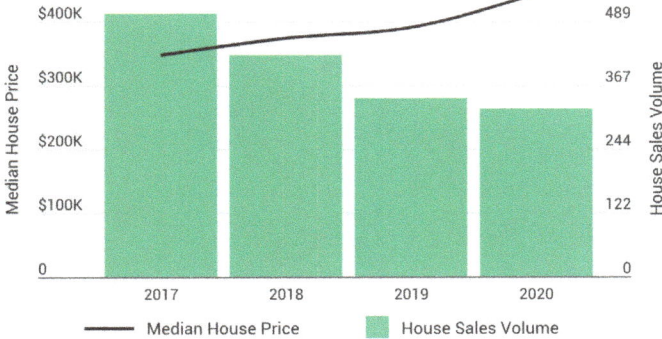

Median House Price · House Sales Volume

Source: Domain Insight | Prepared by InvestorKit

We can see that the house prices of Caboolture grew by 27% over those same three years, which disproves the myth that declining sales volumes lead to poor-value growth.

There's never one factor that can be examined in isolation to indicate the market trends. The more data you read, the clearer you'll see the market.

WHAT DOES THE DATA SHOW?

This is an interest rate example looking at the RBA cash rate trend over the past 20 years compared with six capital cities' house price trends.

RBA Cash Rate vs 6 Cities' Median House Price Trends
2004–2024

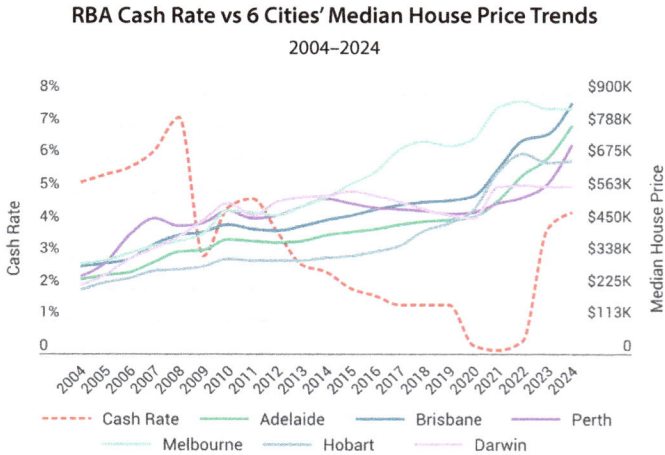

Source: RBA; Domain Insight | Prepared by InvestorKit

You can see that in 2009–10, while the RBA cash rate was trending upward, house prices in all six cities increased. Also, in 2022–24, while the RBA cash rate surged to the highest level since 2011, house prices in Adelaide, Brisbane and Perth achieved extremely strong growth. This disproves the myth that rising interest rates will lead to price declines everywhere.

Chapter 6

MYTHS ABOUT OPPORTUNITIES

I've left this group of myths till last because it relates to mindset more than the market. Often anything to do with the way we learn and think can be the hardest to shift, and when it comes to the property market, there's a lot of noise around when to make your move and what you should and shouldn't do around 'the deal'.

Opportunities also mean options beyond houses and markets. They include other investment possibilities, such as property development, sub-divisions or renovations. As always, it's best to seek the advice of a professional or, best still, lean into your team of investment experts. Sometimes an opportunity leads to success, but you need to see through the noise first as you'll see in this chapter.

Here are the myths we'll bust in this chapter:

1. *Everyone thinks it's all about the deal.*

2. *Everyone thinks development potentials are good for your portfolio.*

3. *Everyone thinks buying apartments is the best first property to buy.*

4. *Everyone thinks you have to invest as early as possible.*

1. Everyone thinks it's all about the deal.

When it comes to myths about opportunities, this is another one I hear all the time: the price you pay for a property will affect the profit you make on the other end.

Specifically, the myth is that the better the deal (a cheaper price or higher vendor discount), the more profit (capital growth) you'll take.

WHAT DOES THE DATA SHOW?

Let's look at a regional New South Wales example. There are two New South Wales regions shown below. If you were to choose one to buy back in 2014, which one would you choose?

Upper Hunter vs Lower Hunter

SA3	Median Price 2014	Vendor Discount 2014
Upper Hunter	$300,000	4.0%
Lower Hunter	$315,000	2.5%

Source: Domain Insight | Prepared by InvestorKit

If you were after a better deal, Upper Hunter looks better because it had a slightly lower price and a higher likely vendor discount rate. However, in the eight years since then, Lower Hunter's house prices grew much more strongly than Upper Hunter, as you can see in the next chart.

Strong growth doesn't happen due to a better negotiated deal or a low initial price, but due to high market pressure.

Upper Hunter and Lower Hunter Median House Price Trends
2014–2022

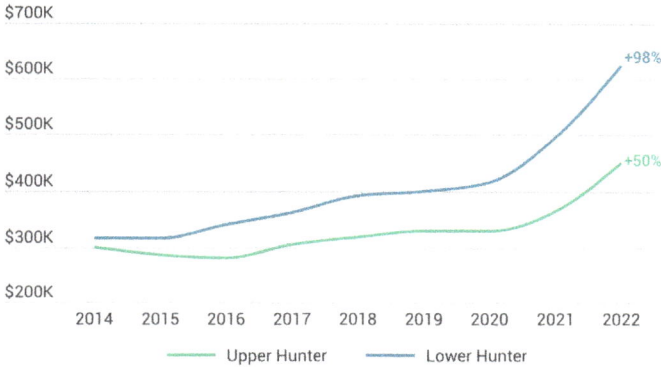

Source: Domain Insight | Prepared by InvestorKit

Inventory (the ratio between the total number of listings at a
point in time and the monthly sales volume) is one of the best
indicators of market pressure. The following chart shows that
Upper Hunter inventory was much higher than Lower Hunter
in 2014–15, leading to much weaker growth in the following
few years.

Upper Hunter and Lower Hunter Inventory Trends
2014–2022

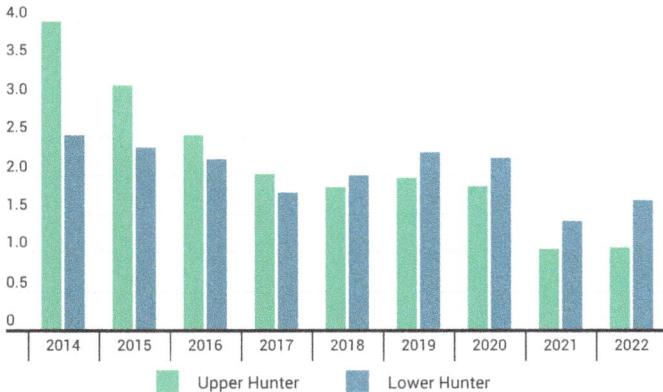

Source: Domain Insight | Prepared by InvestorKit

2. Everyone thinks development potentials are good for your portfolio.

For some investors who've had success with single-dwelling apartments or houses, the next opportunity might be to invest in a property with development potential. The idea of snapping up a big block and subdividing it to hopefully double, triple or even quadruple your profit sounds appealing, doesn't it?

But these opportunities are less common than you might think, because developing property is incredibly complex and challenging. It should only be tackled if you're extremely comfortable and understand what you're getting into, and can lean into the expertise and support of a team not just experienced in property but specifically property development and all the legal, finance and legislation ramifications. Property development is a business you need to run well and not simply an 'investment' you can sit on. Developing comes with:

- *High costs.* Property development involves significant costs, including construction expenses, labour and fees.
- *Building costs.* Australia's construction costs have surged significantly since 2021 as both material and labour supply chains were disturbed by the pandemic. The chart shows the indexed trend of construction costs in Australia.

House Construction Inputs Index Trend in Australia
2018–2023

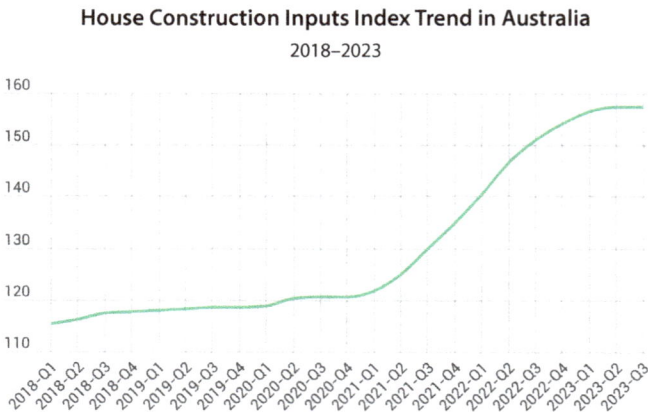

Source: ABS | Prepared by InvestorKit

- *Delay risks.* This is a huge – and often unavoidable – part of development investment. There can be delays in construction, material supply, labour, finances, councils, or a combination of all these. Before the pandemic, it usually took six months to complete a new house – the commencement and completion lines align with a six-month lag. However, the commencement–completion balance has been broken since 2020, suggesting that a huge number of dwellings are being completed longer than six months after commencement.

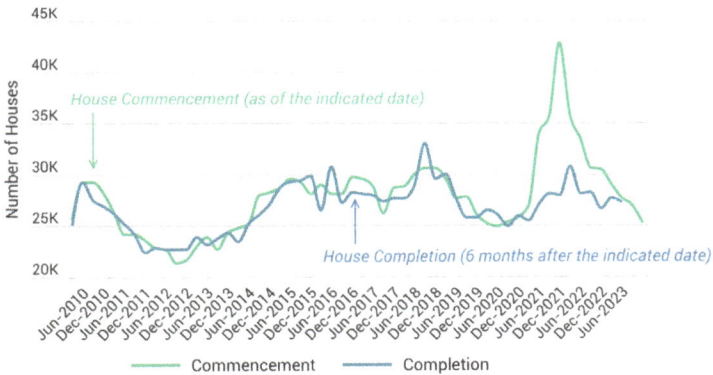

Australia House Construction Commencement vs Completions
2010–2023 (with 6 months' lag)

Source: ABS | Prepared by InvestorKit

- *Regulation problems.* There are also issues around regulations, which can add considerable cost when plans run awry. Even if you do have your Development Approval (DA) in order, real estate market changes can affect your timing and profits. Suddenly, the property you developed and finished can't be sold at a price high enough to recover your costs because the market has changed and cooled down.

Finally, if you do buy a house with development potential and rent it out, you may risk a low yield, especially if the purchase price is high due to the cost of the land. It can be tricky to achieve a high enough rental price to match your rental return expectation. And while you hold the property, do you want to keep managing its upkeep? It's unlikely that a home with development potential is well kept because the seller would have realised the same potential. But they decided not to do any improvements on the place over time.

Personally, I've been able to build my $17 million+ portfolio with zero properties that hold development potential. I didn't want any pressure to develop with such low odds of success and so much that could potentially work against me. I'm not saying it can't work or doesn't happen; I'm simply saying why not achieve greater returns than the majority who go down the development path without success, without the risks and complexity?

3. Everyone thinks buying apartments is the best first property to buy.

In some of our most expensive Australian cities – for example, Sydney and Gold Coast – it's becoming increasingly difficult to jump onto the property ladder. I see many buyers who wish to get started but without the budget for a house think an apartment is the next best thing.

They feel comfortable buying in their own city (or their own neighbourhood) and want something that looks nice. But with their limited budget, they'll often buy an off-the-plan apartment or even one online that's built and ready to go.

What they have overlooked is that if they invest borderless, they can buy a house that generates a similar rental return and grows much more in value. While in earlier myths we did cover houses vs apartments, I want to revisit this because so many people think apartments should be their first investment before they transition to a house over time. It's crazy! There are so many locations across the country where houses are still affordable and generate good rental returns.

As at the end of 2024:

- There were 23 SA3s in New South Wales where the median house prices was still under $650,000. All are regional cities.

- The median house price of Townsville, a regional hub in North Queensland, was $516,000, growing 23% in a year.

- The median house price of Playford, an SA3 40 km north of Adelaide CBD, was $560,000, growing 24% in a year.

All of these options have substantially outperformed apartment growth and offer affordable entry prices for many.

WHAT DOES THE DATA SHOW?

Here are three properties that were sold 10 years ago and then sold again lately. Their growth is fantastic:

Apartments vs Houses
2012–2022

#	Address	2011/12 Sale	2021/22 Sale	10-Year Growth	Estimated Rent 2022
1	70X/8X Shoreline Drive Rhodes, NSW (Apartment, 2bed–2bath–1car)	Apr 2012 $619K (off the plan)	Jan 2022 $950K	53.5%	$650/w
2	3X Hillcrest Street Wollongong, NSW (House, 4bed–3bath–2car)	Mar 2012 $670K	Oct 2021 $1,460K	117.9%	$950/w
3	2X Seville Road Holland Park, QLD (House, 4bed–3bath–3car)	Dec 2011 $570K	Nov 2021 $1,215K	113.2%	$750/w

Source: RP Data | Prepared by InvestorKit

So, if you're planning to invest in an off-the-plan apartment just because you can't afford a house in your comfort zone, whether it's your suburb, your city or your state, look beyond your borders first.

4. Everyone thinks you have to invest as early as possible.

I've met many first-time investors in their forties and beyond who regret not entering the market earlier to enjoy more years of compound growth. Looking ahead, they worry they don't have enough time before retirement too.

So, is it too late to start investing? No!

The beauty of starting your investment journey after 40 is that you're more likely to have a secure financial position with high savings, well-established careers, healthy equity in your family home if you have one and likely fewer debt burdens. This provides a stronger foundation for property investments.

The data proves it too.

WHAT DOES THE DATA SHOW?

According to the ABS, the 45–54 age group is the highest-earning group, with an average weekly income of $2,235 for a full-time worker ($116,220 annually).

Australian Average Weekly Earnings by Age Group
Full-time Employees, 2023

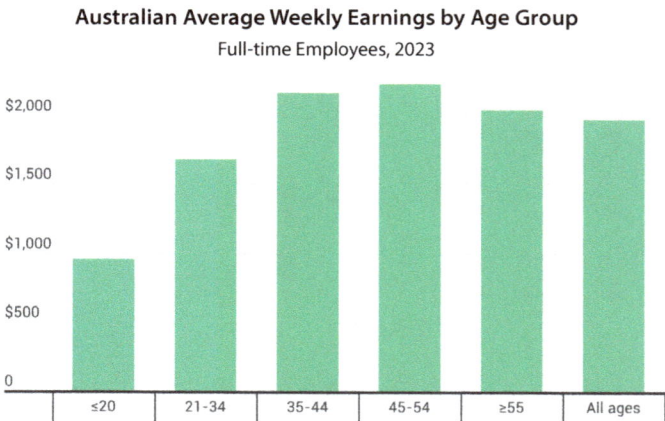

Source: ABS | Prepared by InvestorKit

Savings increase as we age, too. This is shown in the next chart, which shows the average savings amount of Westpac customers by age group. Note the clear climb between 35–44 and 45–54, which is more evidence that you're likely to be able to save faster than younger investors.

Westpac Clients Average Savings by Age Group
2024

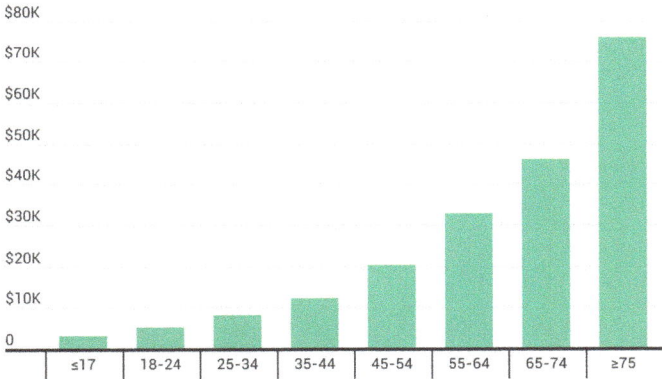

Source: Westpac | Prepared by InvestorKit

The research also shows that financial experience and literacy are positively correlated with age, and with richer experience and better decision-making abilities, you could be much more efficient in reaching your wealth-building goal in later years than 10 or 20 years ago.

Finally, when you know your wealth-building deadline (your retirement age target) is approaching, you may feel more pressure to diligently save and invest and so will likely progress faster.

TL:DR 3 TIPS

There were a lot of myths to bust in this part, and while I live and breathe this, I also appreciate that it's a lot of data to digest. So, if I were to pull out the three most important lessons, these are the easiest to share when it comes to dispelling the chatter among friends and family:

1. Don't use a single indicator or news source.

2. Don't insist on buying in your own backyard.

3. You don't have to choose between timing the market and time in the market.

* * *

Next, we're going to move on to the second part of the book. This is all about setting you up with the right information and tools so that you can make more informed decisions. If this part was about myths, the next is about fundamentals. Unlearning, and now learning.

Let's go!

Grab Your Free Bonus Resources!

Enjoying the book? Head to **www.investorkit.com.au/book-resources** to unlock your exclusive bonus materials, tools, indicators and templates designed to help you take action and get results.

Don't miss out – they're free and ready for you now!

PART II
FUNDAMENTALS

How are you feeling? Were there a few myths that you swore by but now can see are founded on fallacies? Don't worry – that was me too in your shoes many years ago, listening to my family and 'experts' tell me what they thought was true. As I mentioned, listening to them cost me dearly but I made it my mission to start unlearning and get smarter.

It can be hard to undo years of property programming and replace theories you thought were sound with something different altogether. It can also be hard to read about myths commonly quoted in the media as fact by other 'property professionals'. You may be feeling confused as to who's right!

But I want you to take comfort in the numbers. Hopefully, you understood how I unpacked the myths, and the data I applied is starting to make sense. Up next is where I take you through the 'right' learnings, and there's no better place to start than with the property fundamentals.

In part II, I'll take you through what I consider to be the three core fundamentals. No myths, no assumptions, just the absolute foundations of the property market that will give you the basis for how to move on to make informed property investment decisions.

Chapter 7

WHAT ARE THE PROPERTY FUNDAMENTALS?

I t might seem obvious to include a section about fundamentals. Firstly, I'm here because I want to make an important point about the way property data is collected and collated, because this has an overall impact on the way we understand it.

My problem with reading and understanding the property news is that whenever anything is reported on property investing, you often hear about it at a country level. From median prices to auction results, property data is often quoted across the nation – even though you are buying a house on a street in a suburb in a town or city in a state in the country. You don't *buy* the 'country' when you buy a 'property'.

As a result, the data doesn't represent you, because yes, you live in Australia (or elsewhere around the globe!) but nation-wide data is too broad to be relevant specifically to you. The mainstream media uses reports and numbers for their audience – predominantly the 10 to 12 million people in Sydney and Melbourne and surrounds. This means that Australian data is largely weighted by two cities representing the whole country, so you'll only ever get country-level information largely moulded by these two areas, rather than data that is more reflective of each place and market, providing you with a complete picture of what is really driving housing price growth or price declines.

Secondly, the same data and metrics used by the media are packaged in isolation to be quick and snappy. They do this to attract more readers or viewers for themselves; for example, by using rental data in isolation to illustrate the housing crisis or migration data for the same purpose because they only have a few minutes in a news segment or a 400-word article.

The problem is that these quick hits are an oversimplified review of data. You come to think that this one data point rules, or that one data point makes everything happen. News that doesn't make sense to the majority, and news that is isolated, will trap you and put you in paralysis by analysis.

Now, let's talk about the fundamentals instead. The fundamentals are the key drivers of the property market. The 'real' way the market moves. By understanding these, you'll be able to assess the information you read or hear every day in a much more informed way. I've broken this down into three areas that drive the property market. These are:

- demand
- supply
- confidence ...

along with their influencers.

Spread across these three drivers are 26 indicators – or metrics – that are the hard data providing the evidence supporting the influencers. All of these indicators are easily accessible and available to you to discover and unpack. No more relying on websites or newspaper articles! In this part, I'll take you through each of the three drivers and the metrics that relate to them, which ones are more important than others, and how these shape the whole country.

Why is this important? When you consider the right metrics, you'll make much more informed decisions about what's happening in the country. It won't necessarily give you the right strategy to help you buy a house (that's another book for another day!), but it will block all the noise and give you a strong source of truth. With truth comes power, and the sense to know what is truly happening in the market, plus the risks, dangers and opportunities moving forward so that you can make your own well-informed decisions.

Now, let's learn more about our three drivers and indicators.

Chapter 8

DEMAND

I n its simplest property terms, our first driver – demand – relates
to the number of people who are willing and able to buy or
invest. As more and more buyers or investors enter the market,
demand increases, which puts pressure on supply.

But how do you measure demand? After all, the property market is a complex system and prices are hard to predict. I've put it
down to four influencers, which I believe are the most important
determiners of what's creating pressure in the market.

THE FOUR KEY DEMAND INFLUENCERS

As I mentioned, each driver contains a number of influencers, and
there are 26 metrics or indicators that provide the rich data on
each. Understand these and you'll be well on your way towards
better property decisions.

The four key demand influencers are:

1. *People movement:* The more people there are relative to supply,
   the higher the housing demand.

2. *Economic activity:* The more active the economy, the higher the demand.

3. *Finance:* The easier it is to borrow, the higher the demand.

4. *Affordability:* The more affordable property is relative to incomes, the higher the demand.

Now, let's take a deeper look at these demand influencers and the indicators that relate to each.

1. People movement

It makes sense that people are at the centre of housing demand. The first thing anyone does when they move to a new location is find somewhere to live, whether to rent or to buy.

In this influencer, we look at population growth trends, internal and overseas migration trends, household sizes, visitor numbers, and more. This data gives us the best information about where people are moving, which is a strong indicator of where to find demand in the property market.

People movement is not just about overseas migration. People movement comes in all shapes and sizes, including:

- *Household size reduction:* This can relate to kids moving out of home, parents moving out and divorces. All of these create more housing requirements, despite the population remaining the same.

- *Births and deaths:* These can shape household movements and demand for different property types.

- *Regional migration:* People move for lifestyle or job reasons, creating pressure in markets they're moving to and decreasing pressure in markets they're leaving.

- *International visitors:* This positively impacts Airbnb demand, tourism and economic prosperity.

These impact housing markets more than overseas migration does because migrants often rent to begin with and do not purchase for many years. This holistic view of population trends is how you can uncover real demand.

Indicators

The metrics and data we refer to that covers all of the above people movements are:

- *Population growth:* https://www.abs.gov.au/statistics/ people/population/national-state-and-territory-population/ dec-2022#key-statistics

- *Population projection:* https://population.gov.au/data-and-forecasts/projections

- *Net overseas migration:* https://www.abs.gov.au/statistics/ people/population/national-state-and-territory-population/ dec-2022#key-statistics

- *Regional migration*: https://www.regionalaustralia.org.au/ Regional-Movers-Index?hkey=6eb5f956-9bf0-4f2d-8ce7-10cca8387a7c

- *International visitors*: https://www.abs.gov.au/statistics/ people/population/national-state-and-territory-population/ dec-2022#key-statistics

- *Household size*: https://www.rba.gov.au/speeches/2024/sp-ag-2024-05-16.html

Scan here for a complete list of indicators mentioned in this book.

Let's use Hobart's internal migration as an example to show how people movement influences the property market.

WHAT DOES THE DATA SHOW?

You can see in the chart below that Hobart saw an internal migration surge in the few years leading up to 2017, which remained high until the pandemic border closures.

At the same time, Hobart's house prices started an extensive period of solid growth. From 2015 to 2020, the median price increased by 55%, averaging 9.2% annually. This figure may seem nothing compared to the 30%+ surge in 2021 (the COVID property boom) but it's rare for any city to maintain a close-to-double-digit growth rate for so many years.

Greater Hobart Net Internal Migration vs House Price Trend
2013–2023

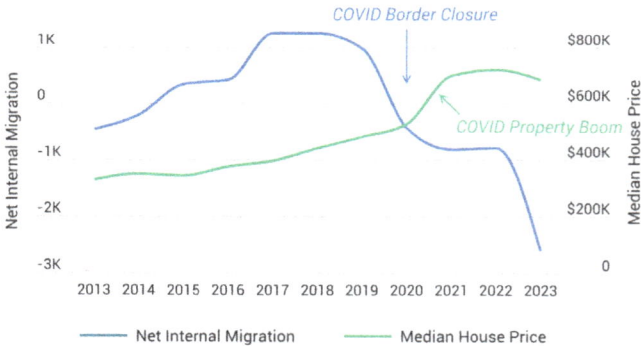

Source: ABS | Prepared by InvestorKit

By reviewing the numbers, we can see that the increasing housing demand from the internal migration surge contributed significantly to this outstanding performance. However, in isolation no one indicator will do all the heavy lifting. This example is to illustrate it can play a key part if other points come together.

ARJUN'S INSIGHT

Always consider population data in line with supply, as population growth when met with an availability of houses for rent and/or sale can easily be accommodated and in turn reduce market heat. Population growth isn't as important as population pressure.

2. Economic activity

The local economy influences property market demand by boosting or suppressing buyers' confidence and purchasing power. In a thriving economy, more people have stable jobs and increasing incomes and are, therefore, willing to borrow from the bank for large items like cars or properties. On the other hand, in a sluggish economy, more people are unemployed or underemployed or don't expect income to grow and are, therefore, more reluctant to make any significant purchases.

In this category, we typically look at GDP growth (GRP for cities or regions), unemployment rates, job advertisements, infrastructure investment and commodity prices (especially for mining-driven economies).

Indicators

To accurately see how the economy is impacting the property market, we look at these metrics:

- *GDP growth*: https://business.nab.com.au/australian-economic-update-q1-gdp-2023-60578/

- *Unemployment rate/job advertisements*: https://www.abs.gov.au/statistics/labour/employment-and-unemployment/labour-force-australia-detailed/latest-release;
  https://www.jobsandskills.gov.au/data

- *Infrastructure investment*: https://www.infrastructureaustralia. gov.au/infrastructure-market-capacity-program

- *Commodity prices and exports*: https://www.rba.gov.au/ statistics/frequency/commodity-prices/2023/icp-0623.html

Scan here for a complete list of indicators mentioned in this book.

Let's see how Townsville's local property market trends moved with the improving economy.

WHAT DOES THE DATA SHOW?

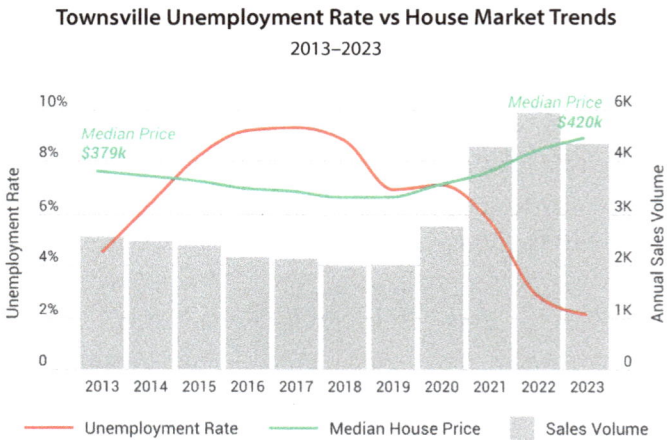

Townsville Unemployment Rate vs House Market Trends
2013–2023

Source: ABS; Domain Insight | Prepared by InvestorKit

Townsville's unemployment rates started rising in the early 2010s as the mining boom ended, reaching its peak of almost 10% in early 2017. The surging unemployment rate was accompanied by decreasing house sales volume and house prices.

From 2017 to 2019, Townsville's local economy was gradually regaining strength. However, while the unemployment rate was declining, it was still relatively high, indicating that there weren't enough jobs to attract people back to the city or the property market, thus the low sales volume and house prices.

It was in 2020 that things started to change: the economy continued recovering, offering more and more job opportunities, and the unemployment rate, after a brief increase due to the initial shock of the pandemic, started to decline steeply. The exodus-to-affordability-and-lifestyle trend emerging in the pandemic helped bring more residents, visitors and property investors to the city, further boosting the economy and housing market demand.

As a result of all these factors working together, Townsville's house price growth has been accelerating since 2021.

During this time Townsville also received support at a state and federal level via the 'city deal'. Billions of dollars in infrastructure spending supported the city through its transformation, with a key landmark being the new rugby league stadium for the North Queensland Cowboys team.

ARJUN'S INSIGHT

When looking at economic activity, the unemployment rate is a great data resource, especially when coupled with increasing job ads, rising wages and a healthy infrastructure pipeline. This increases local purchasing power capability, housing demand and local confidence.

3. Finance

Finance is the third demand influencer. I've included this in demand because most people, especially investors, need finance (a loan) to buy a property.

When finance is easy, property market demand is high or increasing. An example is the COVID property boom, which was boosted by historically low interest rates and an unprecedentedly high household saving ratio.

From a lending point of view, finance has two aspects. One is a supply factor (the availability of finance), and the other is demand (the take-up of that availability).

Indicators

There are a few metrics we can use to see how finances affect the property market. In this category, we consider the RBA cash rate, household income growth, household savings ratio, new loan commitment number and value, residential loan-to-value ratio, bank delinquency rate and borrowing capacity.

- *Cash rate:* https://www.rba.gov.au/

- *Household income:* https://www.abs.gov.au/statistics/economy/price-indexes-and-inflation/wage-price-index-australia/mar-2023

- *Household saving ratio:* https://www.rba.gov.au/chart-pack/

- *New loan commitments:* https://www.abs.gov.au/statistics/economy/finance/lending-indicators/latest-release

- *Residential loan-to-value ratio:* https://www.corelogic.com.au/news-research/reports/monthly-housing-chart-pack

- *Bank delinquency rate:* https://www.apra.gov.au/news-and-publications/apra-releases-quarterly-authorised-deposit-taking-institution-statistics-19; https://www.rba.gov.au/chart-pack/

Demand

- *Borrowing capacity:* https://www.commbank.com.au/digital/home-loans/calculator/how-much-can-i-borrow

Scan here for a complete list of indicators mentioned in this book.

WHAT DOES THE DATA SHOW?

Let's focus on the new loan commitment number. This is a metric that measures how many people in the market are taking out new loans. It's a great indicator of housing market confidence and demand.

In late 2020, the RBA cash rate kept dropping. The initial shock of the pandemic had passed and households' saving ratios surged. People began to feel more comfortable borrowing money and making significant purchases; for example, houses. That's when we saw a boom in new home loan commitments nationwide. The following chart shows what happened in NSW.

Number of Home Loan Commitment vs Indexed House Price Trends
Greater Sydney vs Regional NSW, 2019–2023 (2019 = 1.0)

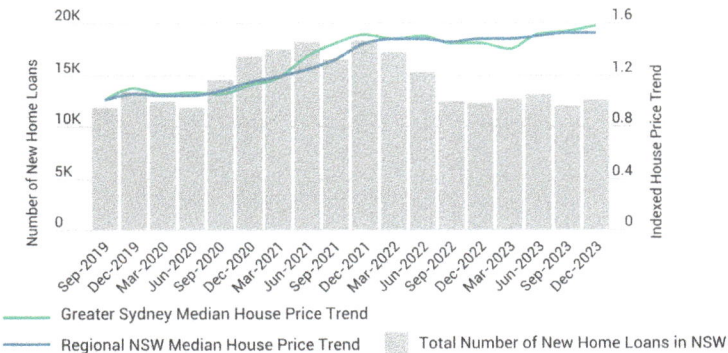

Source: ABS | Prepared by InvestorKit

The number of new home loans in New South Wales started surging in September 2020, indicating booming housing demand and high buyer confidence. Following that, house prices in both Sydney and regional New South Wales started growing fast in the December quarter.

In early 2022, signs of cash rate hikes had emerged. The banks became more prudent in lending, and people became more reluctant to borrow. As a result, their borrowing capacity shrank, there was a decrease in new home loans and ultimately weaker demand in the property market. As demand declined sharply in 2022, house prices in both Sydney and regional New South Wales also went into decline, although to different extents.

ARJUN'S INSIGHT

Not all markets react to finance changes the same way; some are more sensitive, as evidenced by many parts of New South Wales following these finance trend lines. In more affordable markets between 2022 and 2024 such as Perth, Adelaide and regional Queensland, finance numbers weakened even as demand was still high due to supply levels being critically low of houses for sale and for rent!

4. Affordability

Housing affordability is always an essential factor for people to consider when they decide where to live and work. While high affordability doesn't necessarily mean high demand, it contributes positively to housing demand if the other influencers also trend well.

Indicators

In this demand category, we look at the following three metrics:

- *Rental affordability:* https://www.anz.com.au/newsroom/news/2024/april/anz-news-corelogic-housing-affordability-report/

- *Mortgage affordability:* https://www.anz.com.au/newsroom/news/2024/april/anz-news-corelogic-housing-affordability-report/

- *Price to income ratio:* https://www.corelogic.com.au/__data/assets/pdf_file/0016/23191/CoreLogic-HVI-JUL-2024-FINAL.pdf

WHAT DOES THE DATA SHOW?

This chart shows how affordability affects housing demand and price growth when mortgage interest rates increase dramatically.

Australian SA3s Median House Price Level vs Growth in an Interest-Rate-Hiking Period

May 2022–Nov 2023

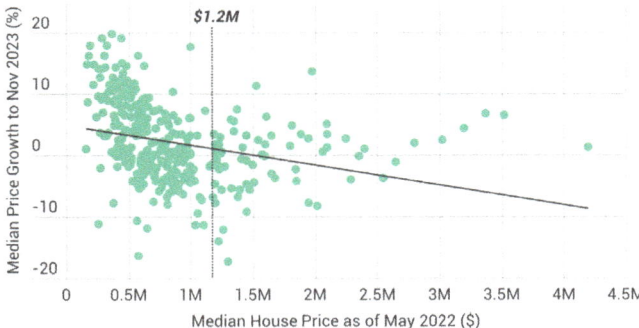

Source: Domain Insight | Prepared by InvestorKit

The RBA cash rate hikes started in May 2022 and stopped in Nov 2023, becoming the steepest rate rise in history. How did Australian regions' house prices grow over the same period?

As shown, 80% of Australia's SA3 regions had median house prices lower than $1.2 million. For these regions, a significant negative correlation between price level and growth rate over the period can be seen – the more affordable, the higher the growth.

However, for those regions with a median price above $1.2 million, especially various sought-after regions in Sydney, Melbourne and southeast Queensland, the negative correlation has become negligible. It's likely that one or more other factors, rather than mortgage affordability, have a stronger influence on those cities' housing demand.

For example, their location supply levels are tight, there is greater buyer bias, preference and dependence level on bank loans (the bank of mum and dad has become more common in high-price markets) and there are many properties that often trade in cash.

It's also important to note that mortgage affordability's influence on demand and price growth is not always as significant as in the past 1.5 years (at the time of writing). In times of stable or low interest rates, the negative correlation we see above would be unnoticeable. Instead, other factors would take over and have more influence on the property market.

ARJUN'S INSIGHT

At the end of the day, if a purchase takes place anywhere it can be – technically – deemed 'affordable', while it's not popular to say so. If either finance was approved using Australia's conservative finance providers with many buffers and strenuous checks in place, or it was purchased with a high amount of cash, these measures simply provide different viewpoints of affordability.

CASE STUDY

Cameron Galloway – InvestorKit client

Cameron is a vice president at a major financial group. As a finance professional, he is analytical but time poor, and values expertise and the power of building a team around him. His core goal was to build his wealth first so that he could set up his future. Applying the property fundamentals, Cameron's strategy was to purchase all three of his properties at the right point of growth cycles using data and where possible off-market, which enabled him to secure affordable prices and high yields. He continues to unlock equity in his portfolio and is looking to buy a fifth property.

Before

As a rentvestor, Cameron's focus was to build capital. He'd delayed buying a home so he could build his wealth first, which he did so successfully for several years. But as a senior professional he lacked the time to research and find a property, let alone take the plunge and buy one.

The process

To fast-track Cameron into his first purchase, our strategy was to create a combination of early-adopter and hotspot markets (we will unpack these cycle stages later in the book). It was also important to seek industry and city diversity across his portfolio.

We purchased three properties for him, each off-market across South Australia and Queensland. The first two, in Adelaide and Townsville in regional Queensland, were purchased at the earlier parts of the market cycles at affordable prices and high yields, while the third was a classic hotspot in Toowoomba, Queensland. All demonstrated a strong application of the fundamentals of affordability, diversity across states and diversity across market cycles.

What's important to note about Cameron's portfolio is that the first property was purchased in 2020, when the world was first experiencing the pandemic. We knew that going into COVID supply was severely impacted, demand was being injected with a lot of government stimulus, and there was a lot of job loss and unemployment. However, we also knew that a single world event isn't long-lasting and that once things got back to normality, the market would also show some positive signs.

Unlike the myths, Cameron didn't acknowledge the doom and gloom in the news but instead used his understanding of the property fundamentals to guide him towards sound investment decisions.

The result

Cameron's portfolio now includes more than $2 million in compounding assets with nearly $800,000 in equity growth – from just three properties. Despite challenging periods including the pandemic, low sentiment and rising interest rates, he stayed the course and never swayed from his goals.

He's constantly reviewing his portfolio and planning to unlock equity and purchase a fourth property with his partner in the near future. Then, we'll take a step back and consider high cashflow commercial assets on his fifth and potentially more. Go Cameron!

Cameron's property journey

- **Property 1:** Modbury North, Adelaide, 2020 for $468,000

  Today's value: $820,000 (75.20%)

- **Property 2:** Kearneys Spring, Regional Queensland, 2021 for $590,000

  Today's value: $840,000 (42.37%)

- **Property 3:** Douglas, Regional Queensland, 2022 for $497,500

  Today's value: $655,000 (31.66%)

Total equity growth: $759,500
Total portfolio value: $2.315 million

Now, you can see how the four types of demand fundamentals impact the Australian property market – people movement, economic activity, finance and affordability – and the metrics that I use that influence demand in various ways.

We're ready to move on to supply.

Chapter 9

SUPPLY

If you studied economics like I did, one of the first principles you would have learned was the effect of supply and demand. You can't have one without the other, and for every movement in one is a direct impact on the other. Together, they're intrinsic to the property market.

To meet demand, there must be supply, and this is our second driver.

While we started with the demand influencers – people movement, economic activity, finance and affordability – the truth is that demand wouldn't exist without supply. The desire to own or invest in real estate hinges directly on the availability of properties to meet that demand. Supply dynamics significantly influence market trends, impacting everything from affordability to rental income cashflow.

Unlike demand and its four influencers, supply is influenced by only two factors, along with its corresponding metrics:

1. *Current supply:* The established number of properties already in the market for rent or for sale.

2. *Incoming supply:* The number of future properties to come into the market.

Let's dig deeper.

1. Current supply

The quantity of homes on the market at any given time provides an immediate insight into supply levels. The higher the number of listings for sale or rent, the more bargaining power for buyers and renters. Therefore, prices take their time to rise.

We use two metrics to measure current supply.

Indicators

*   *For-sale listings:* https://sqmresearch.com.au/total-property-listings.php

*   *Rental vacancy rate*: https://sqmresearch.com.au/graph_vacancy.php

WHAT DOES THE DATA SHOW?

The number of 'for-sale listings' indicates the current state of supply in the sales market. Likewise, when considering the rental market, rental vacancy rates are an indicator of current supply.

Imagine a scenario where the number of listings and sales are both going up, and the number of sales is rising faster. The market is tightening despite the increase in the number of listings.

The following chart shows Perth's journey over the past decade, and looks at the dynamics between established supply (number of listings) and demand (number of sales). It's a great way to see how established supply and demand interact and influence price growth.

Greater Perth Number of Listings, Number of Sales vs House Price Trends
2013–2023

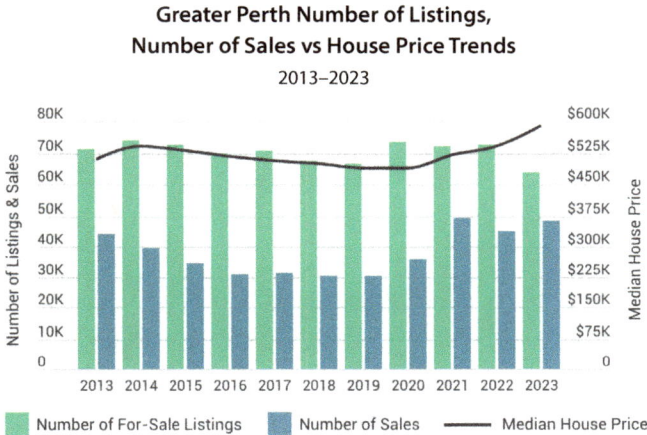

Source: Domain Insight | Prepared by InvestorKit

From 2014 to 2016, Perth's housing market was cooling. The supply (number of listings) was declining but remained high, while demand (number of sales) fell at a faster rate due to the end of the mining boom. You can observe that the gap between supply and demand widened increasingly from 2013, indicating relief from market pressure.

As a result, Perth's house prices started declining in 2014 and maintained a downward trend for six years. Things picked up in 2020, and while the number of for-sale listings stayed high, sales were picking up, closing the gap between supply and demand. Market pressure pushed back up and led house prices to bounce.

Although the surge in demand reduced, the supply level started dropping following 2022, further reducing the difference between supply and demand. The result was that prices continued surging, making Perth the best performer among all capital cities in 2023.

WHAT DOES THE DATA SHOW?

The rental vacancy rate is the primary measure of housing supply in the rental market. Low vacancy rates often indicate a shortage of available rental properties, which can lead to increased competition among renters, so rents are easily pushed up. Likewise, high vacancy rates tend to lead to a renters' market with low market pressure and weak rental growth. I adopt 2% as the high-pressure benchmark for vacancy rates.

Here's a Sydney example of how rental vacancy rates influence rental prices.

Greater Sydney Vacancy Rates vs Asking Rental Price Trends
2010–2024

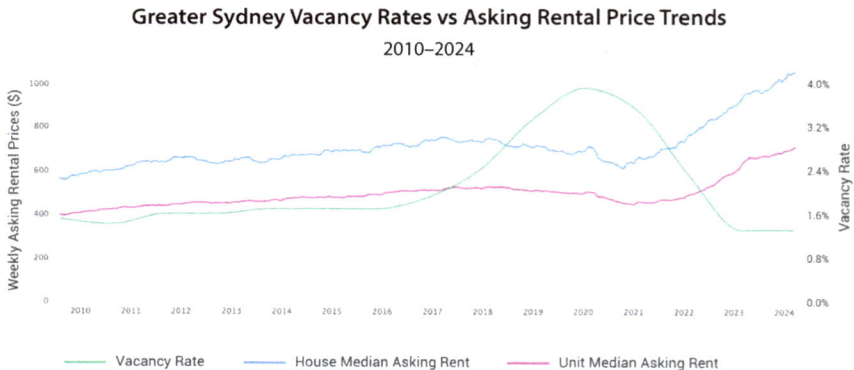

Vacancy Rate ——— House Median Asking Rent ——— Unit Median Asking Rent

Source: SQM Research | Prepared by InvestorKit

Before 2016, Greater Sydney's average rental vacancy rate was relatively low and stable at below 2%, leading to a steady rent increase over those years. However, from 2017 to 2020, vacancy rates surged to higher than 3% due to the vast number of new apartments completed during that period, followed by international border closures in early 2020. As a result, the asking rents of both houses and units declined for four consecutive years (2017 to 2021).

In 2021, as vacancy rates started decreasing steeply, asking prices finally stopped falling and began to increase rapidly. This was the beginning of the rental crisis we are all so familiar with. As at the beginning of 2025, the vacancy rate is still at a historic low range and the rental surge has slowed due to affordability restrictions. I don't see the rental crisis ending anytime soon.

2. Incoming supply

The second influencer on supply is what's coming into the market. Future supply is not as important as established supply, however it's an indicator to consider because too much additional supply may cause slower price growth in the near future if demand can't catch up.

The best way to see this in action is by checking building approvals, and this metric is available from the Australian Bureau of Statistics (ABS). On the website, you can filter your results by type of building, sector of ownership, region and the type of work.

Indicator

• *Building approvals:* https://dataexplorer.abs.gov.au

The following example shows how high-level building approvals can affect growth in Sydney.

WHAT DOES THE DATA SHOW?

Rouse Hill – McGraths Hill and Baulkham Hills are two neighbouring SA3 regions in northwest Sydney. Rouse Hill – McGraths Hill has undergone a large amount of residential development since the 2000s. This chart shows the high building approval figures from 2014 to 2024, while Baulkham Hills has been well established over the same period.

Building Approval Rates vs Indexed House Price Trends
Rouse Hill – McGraths Hill vs Baulkham Hills; 2014–2024 (2014 = 1.00)

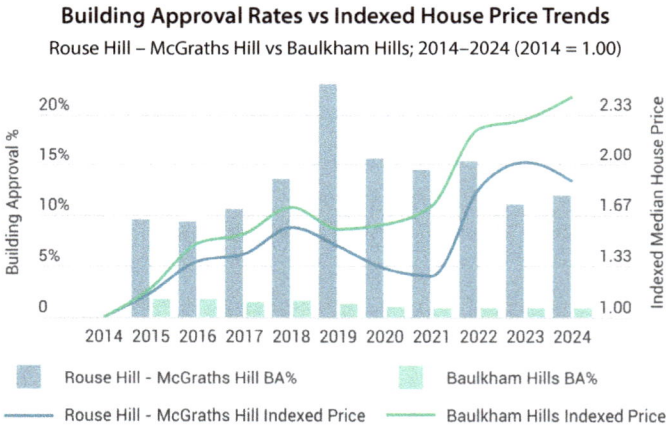

Note: Building Approval % = last 15m total number of building approvals / total number of houses
Source: ABS; Domain Insight | Prepared by InvestorKit

Sydney's property market was booming between 2014 and 2018. House prices rose robustly in both areas, yet Rouse Hill – McGrath Hills didn't perform as well as Baulkham Hills.

In 2018, Sydney's housing market went into recession due to a significant decrease in demand. Almost all suburbs across Sydney saw declining house prices, and this was when the building approval rate showed its influence. With little additional supply, Baulkham's house market showed strong resilience and stopped declining in just one year. By contrast, Rouse Hill – McGrath Hills housing stock surged by 15% to 20% each year, and the excessive supply combined with lower demand led to a three-year price decline in the region.

During the COVID property boom, housing demand was strong, so both regions thrived regardless of their additional housing supply. However, from 2022 to 2024, housing demand declined in Sydney as the RBA cash rate hiked. Baulkham Hills, again with its low supply, didn't see much price drop before regaining growing momentum, while Rouse Hill – McGrath Hills saw a much more notable fall.

To summarise, high incoming supply (building approvals) is fine if demand is strong enough to resolve the fast-growing supply. But when demand is weak, low incoming supply combined with lower established supply equips the market with higher resilience to outperform those with high incoming supply.

Building supply is one of the trickiest to nail and to avoid over-relying on in isolation. As we often see such varied outcomes, some regions can see building supply released very tightly in stages, often with stage-based price increases. Other areas have seen new buildings increase dollar-per-sqm rate premiums, while others have seen strong price declines throughout a suburb for sale and for rent.

ARJUN'S INSIGHT

Looking at supply trends holistically is key. For example, high building approvals will not negatively impact an area if the established building supply and local rental supply is very tight while demand surges. Supply is also one to look at over many years, not just the short term. Today vs long-term trends is what truly paints a clear picture.

Chapter 10

CONFIDENCE

We started with the demand fundamentals – people movement, economic activity, finance and affordability – and the corresponding metrics. Then, we moved on to the supply fundamentals and introduced how established supply and incoming supply influence the market.

Now, we're ready to round out the third piece of the property fundamentals puzzle: confidence!

Confidence is important because it impacts behaviour. If you feel confident in what you're seeing in the market and through your own research (not listening to the barbecue chatter!), you'll be better informed and more likely to make good property decisions.

There are three confidence influencers:

1. *Consumer sentiment:* The level and moving trend of the consumer confidence and sentiment indices not only indicates households' confidence in general spending but also their confidence in spending on housing.

2. *Media cycle:* What the media says has a huge influence on public opinion. If the media appears confident about the property market, the public will be confident too, and vice versa.

3. *Government policies:* Government policies have a profound impact on public confidence. While incentives or encouraging policies boost confidence, suppressive policies damage it.

Now, let's work through these in more detail.

1. Consumer sentiment

Australia has two leading consumer sentiment indices: the *Westpac–Melbourne Institute Consumer Sentiment Index* and the *ANZ–Roy Morgan Consumer Confidence Index*, which are generated through similar surveys. The following table shows the features of each survey.

Consumer Sentiment Surveys Comparison

	Westpac and Melbourne Institute	ANZ-Roy Morgan
Frequency	Monthly (every second Wed)	Weekly (every Tue)
Sample Size	1,200	1,000
Coverage	Residents older than 18 yrs	Residents older than 14 yrs
Interview Method	Over the phone	Face to face
Commenced	1974	1973 (monthly); 2008 (weekly)
Sampling methodology	Stratified to reflect Australian demographics	-

Source: RBA; Westpac and Melbourne Institute; ANZ-Roy Morgan | Prepared by InvestorKit

Indicators

• *Westpac–Melbourne Institute Consumer Sentiment Index:* https://tradingeconomics.com/australia/consumer-confidence

- *ANZ–Roy Morgan Consumer Confidence Index:*
  https://www.roymorgan.com/morgan-poll/consumer-confidence-anz-roy-morgan-australian-cc-summary

The differences in surveying methodology result in different index values; however, the two indices have correlated well over time.

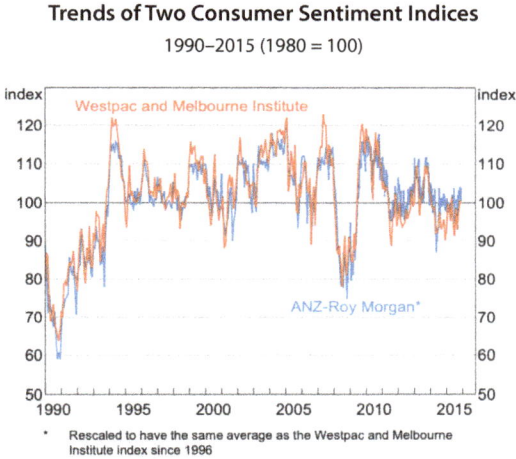

Trends of Two Consumer Sentiment Indices
1990–2015 (1980 = 100)

Westpac and Melbourne Institute

ANZ-Roy Morgan*

* Rescaled to have the same average as the Westpac and Melbourne Institute index since 1996

Source: RBA; Westpac and Melbourne Institute; ANZ-Roy Morgan | Prepared by InvestorKit

Intuitively, consumer confidence links with housing consumer sentiment. When households are confident about their income and wealth, they should be confident in spending on both daily purchases and large items, such as properties.

WHAT DOES THE DATA SHOW?

The following chart shows the relationship between the ANZ–Roy Morgan Consumer Confidence Index and Australia's total dwelling value from 2018 to 2024.

**ANZ–Roy Morgan Consumer Confidence Index
vs Australia's Dwelling Value Growth**

2018–2024

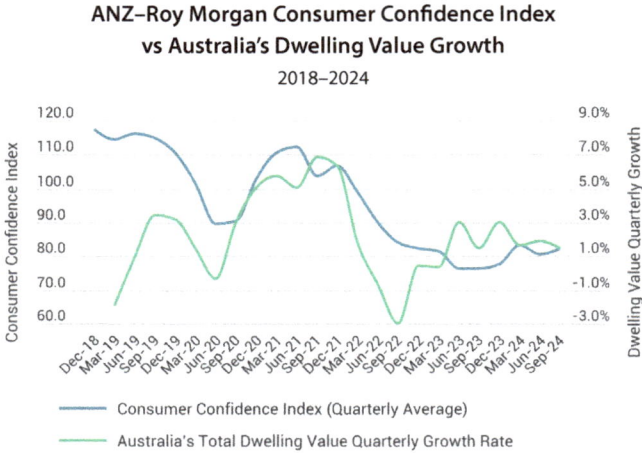

Source: ANZ-Roy Morgan; ABS | Prepared by InvestorKit

From 2018 to early 2020, consumer confidence dropped from 117 to 90, and Australia's dwelling value was declining for much of that period. From 2020 to early 2022, consumer confidence was boosted by government financial support (for example, JobKeeper payment, spending vouchers) and surging household savings. During this period, the property market experienced an unprecedented boom.

From early 2022 to 2023, households were discouraged by high inflation and interest rate hikes. As a result, consumer confidence declined in 2023 to the lowest point in more than 30 years. In the property market, dwelling value declined sharply in 2022, followed by a weak recovery in 2023. It's worth noting that although these were the dangerous *national* trends, they're not the *local* trends you should be following instead.

In 2024, consumer confidence gradually recovered as inflation got under control and interest rates stabilised. This was a good sign that the property market would start gaining more solid growth via confidence. However, again, focus on local market analysis with an improved understanding of the fundamentals.

2. Media cycle

Research shows that the media has a great influence on the public's confidence in the economy. Because of that, there's a lot of noise. Whether through news websites, television, podcasts or radio, the media loves a property story, and I spent some time earlier in the book explaining how articles can be skewed depending on which metric they choose to focus on.

Indicators

- *Media cycle*:
    - https://www.afr.com/property/residential
    - https://www.news.com.au/finance/real-estate
    - https://discover.abc.net.au/

Scan here for a complete list of indicators mentioned in this book.

To measure confidence via the news cycle, I look at news sentiment and how this correlates with consumer sentiment. Let's have a look at some data.

WHAT DOES THE DATA SHOW?

In the next chart we can see this in action – how news sentiment correlates with consumer sentiment (ANZ–Roy Morgan Index). We'll look at this over the past 30 years. It's clear that what we read, hear and watch in the news impacts how we think and feel.

News Sentiment Index vs Consumer Sentiment Index
1988–2020

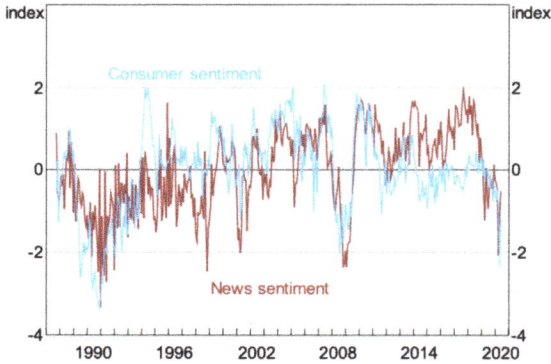

*New Sentiment Index (NSI) is calculated based on the difference between
positive words and negative words used in news articles towards the economy.*

Source: RBA; ANZ-Roy Morgan; Dow Jones Factiva | Prepared by InvestorKit

Similarly, housing news sentiment influences property market performance. In the same RBA research, economists found that in Sydney and Melbourne, Australia's two largest property markets, the local housing news sentiment captures key fluctuations in the local house prices.

Housing News Sentiment Index vs House Prices
Sydney and Melbourne, 1988–2020

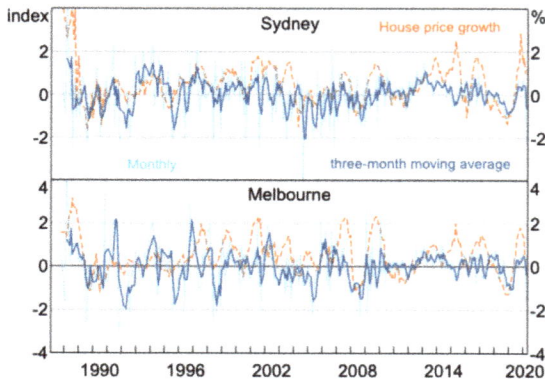

Source: Dow Jones DNA; RBA | Prepared by InvestorKit

At the end of each financial year, InvestorKit undertakes a similar exercise to measure housing news sentiment in Australia. In July 2022, we found that 32.5% of housing market news articles from the three largest media (ABC, AFR and News Corp) were pessimistic about the property market, 24% were positive, and the rest were neutral.

In July 2023, only 17.9% were pessimistic, indicating higher news sentiment. The news sentiment improvement made us believe that Australia's housing market would gain strength in the coming financial year. As expected, price growth started picking up in the second half of 2023.

Trend of Weighted Average of SA3 Median House Prices
Dec 2022–Feb 2024

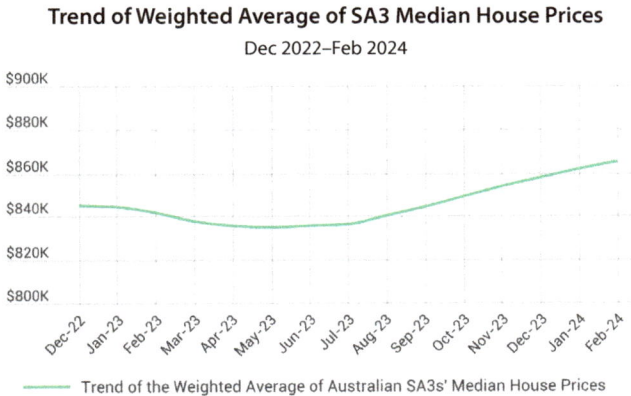

Trend of the Weighted Average of Australian SA3s' Median House Prices

Source: Domain Insight | Prepared by InvestorKit

What this tells us is that what we read in the news has an impact on property prices. It's no surprise that the more pessimistic the news, the less active the market, but remember to keep in mind that the media is in the business of 'selling' news and bad news sells better than good news. Read everything with a grain of salt!

3. Government policies

Another impact on confidence is the government. Government policies and support have a profound impact on public confidence. Similar to the news cycle, incentives or encouraging policies boost confidence, while suppressive policies damage it.

This is supported by historical data, which shows that government incentives or encouraging policies boost property buyers' confidence, and unfavourable policies discourage property buyers.

Indicator

- *Government intervention:* Multiple government websites.

WHAT DOES THE DATA SHOW?

The next chart shows Australia's property market trend in the two decades from 2003 to 2022, with major government policies noted along the journey (green = encouraging; red = discouraging).

You can see that the FHOG Booster and the loosening up of FIRB restrictions in 2008 significantly encouraged owner-occupying buyers, as seen in the big jump in the number of owner-occupier home loan commitments in 2009. However, the removal of these policies two years later brought down the number of these buyers immediately.

Investors were also affected by the government's 2015 and 2017 APRA policies, which were designed to limit investment activities. Both policies immediately suppressed investor confidence, as seen in the decrease in investor loan commitments in 2016 and 2018.

New Loan Commitments by Purchaser Type, Property Market Policies and Median House Price

2003–2022

2003–2022

Oct 2008: First Home Owners Grant Boost is introduced as an addition to the First Home Owners Grant. First Home Savers Accounts are also introduced to improve property market accessibility.

Dec 2008: FIRB rules allow temporary visa holders to more easily buy up second-hand dwellings.

Jan 2010: First Home Owners Grant Boost removed

Apr 2010: Rules allowing foreign investment in real estate that were introduced in 2008 are withdrawn.

Jun 2015: APRA 10% investment credit growth limit introduced

Mar 2017: "A Comprehensive Plan to Address Housing Affordability" initiatives include improving supply, creating incentives, limiting foreign investors' activities, improving social housing, etc.

Mar 2017: APRA limits interest only lending to 30% of new loans.

Mar 2020: APRA suspended much of its planned policy and supervision agenda to prioritise activities to respond to the impacts of COVID-19.

Nov 2020: The Federal government extends the HomeBuilder grants scheme until 31 March 2021 at a reduced rate of $15,000.

GFC

COVID-19

Loan Value: $24,000M, $22,000M, $20,000M, $18,000M, $16,000M, $14,000M, $12,000M, $10,000M, $8,000M, $6,000M, $4,000M, $2,000M, 0

Australian Median House Price: $800K, $733K, $667K, $600K, $533K, $467K, $400K, $333K, $267K, $200K, $133K, $67K, 0

Years: 2003, 2004, 2005, 2006, 2007, 2008, 2009, 2010, 2011, 2012, 2013, 2014, 2015, 2016, 2017, 2018, 2019, 2020, 2021, 2022

Owner Occupier Loan Commitment   Investor Loan Commitment   Australian Median House Price

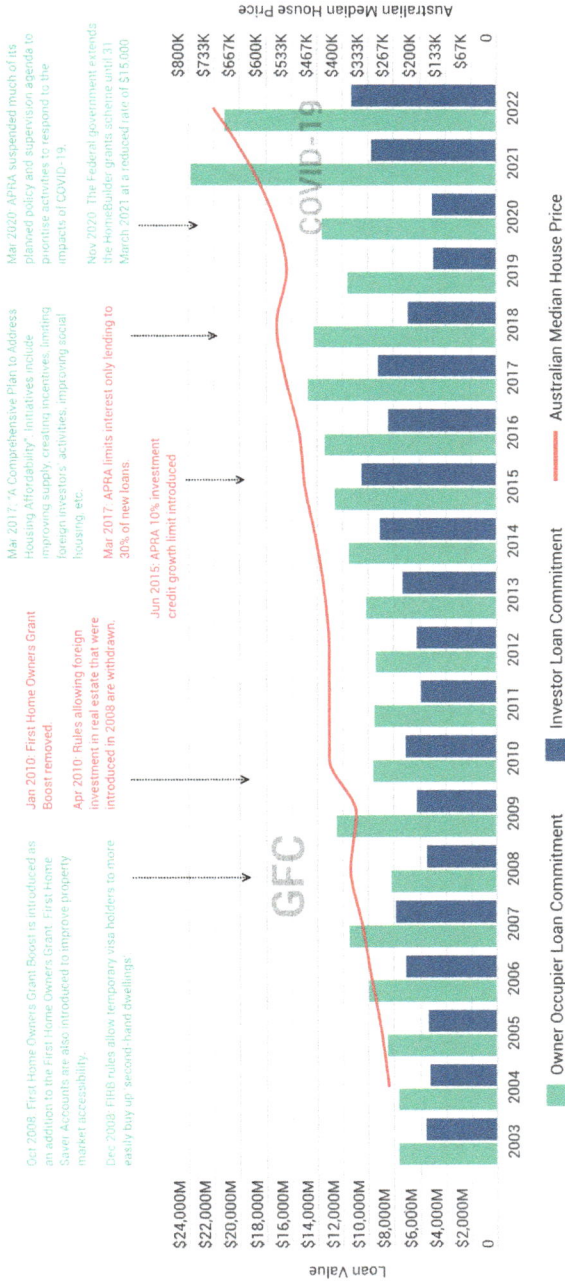

Source: ABS | Prepared by InvestorKit

In 2021, encouraging policies and cash incentives together with historic low interest rates and high household savings boosted both owner-occupier and investor confidence in property purchasing. The numbers for both groups were pushed to the highest levels in over a decade. At the same time, prices skyrocketed, leading to the COVID property boom.

The impact of government policies on the property market can be seen on lower levels as well, as we can see in Victoria. The state's land tax change in 2023 triggered a large number of investors to leave the state. According to local investors, the state's increased land taxes, high council rates and high compliance costs all damaged their confidence in property investment in Victoria.

ARJUN'S INSIGHT

Don't let what you read, watch or hear impact your investing decisions. While it's clear the media impacts the sentiment of many, they can also represent moments to take advantage of lower competition and find the right growth regions.

CASE STUDY

Daniel Thal – InvestorKit client

Daniel and his wife are high-net-worth business owners. Daniel works in IT and together with his wife, Maria, the couple has built a very successful portfolio comprising seven purchases including commercial property across four states in four years totalling $12.52 million.

They're a true success story, overcoming market fluctuations by applying the property fundamentals and capitalising on key investment opportunities to achieve significant growth.

Daniel's ultimate aim was to buy his dream home, and six properties later, he achieved his dream in 2022.

Before

In the beginning, Daniel saw us as his real estate advisory firm. All he'd to do was bring the cash, sort out his lending and sign the papers. He assumed he'd the property fundamentals all worked out, because he already had a booming business and had made multiple property purchases on his own. But, these were starting to work against him. He didn't have a clear strategy, feared he was missing out on good deals, didn't like dealing with real estate agents and was afraid of making mistakes. He was time poor too, and felt it was time to reach out for the right guidance and expertise.

The process

We took Daniel through an aggressive acquisition phase with purchases in quick succession, so we could catch up on lost time and start building a prolific portfolio. We purchased foundational assets, which are properties in major cities to anchor his portfolio (properties one and three in capital cities); momentum assets, which are properties in cities all across the country and borderless without any barriers; straight data (properties five and seven in regional markets); and finally passive assets, which are high-income unit blocks and commercial properties focused largely on income growth (properties two and four).

This delivered for him diversity around Australia along with other benefits including high-growth assets, balanced with other higher yielding assets, high cashflow unit blocks and commercial properties. We applied our knowledge of property fundamentals to create diversity in markets as well as another key point of difference by buying for him at a volatile time in Australia when the world was in the pandemic.

By understanding what was shifting and changing at this time, without leaning into the repetitive news cycle, we were able to position Daniel and Maria into properties that would give them excellent returns and representation across Australia and set them up for life.

The result

Daniel's portfolio now comprises seven properties, and he has engaged us to purchase his eighth. All up, his portfolio will total 11 properties with significant equity and growth, including cashflow (the commercial properties) and equity growth (the residential properties).

He is successfully building his family's future wealth, and found and bought his dream family home in 2022 himself (property six) – a huge high point in his investment and personal life.

In the future, he's gearing up for more assets. With a solid residential portfolio, his next focus will be to continue investing in commercial assets.

Daniel's property journey

- **Property 1:** Banyo, Brisbane, 2020 for $550,000
  Today's value: $1.02 million (85.45%)

- **Property 2:** Kangaroo Flat, Victoria, 2021 for $930,000
  Today's value: Each unit $400,000, $1.2 million total (29.03%)

- **Property 3:** Sheidow Park, Adelaide, 2021 for $790,000
  Today's value: $1.12 million (41.77%)

- **Property 4:** North Murrarie, Brisbane, 2021 for $1.01 million (commercial)

Today's value: $1.2 million

Current rent: $67,000+ GST (6.64% net yield)

- **Property 5:** Bargara, Queensland, 2022 for $641,000

  Today's value: $785,000 (22.47%)

- **Property 6:** Abbotsbury, Sydney, 2022 for $2.601 million

  Today's value: $2.8 million

  (InvestorKit supported with negotiate and secure package only, as this was for the clients to live in)

- **Property 7:** Kearneys Spring, regional Queensland, 2023 for $650,000

  Today's value: $795,000 (22.30%)

Total portfolio value: $12.52 million

Total value of InvestorKit purchases and total equity uplift of InvestorKit purchases: $8.920 million ÷ equity uplift = $1.748 million (conservatively, not including commercial uplift)

TL:DR 3 TIPS

There are three core influencers when it comes to examining property market pressure: demand, supply and confidence. These are your property market fundamentals. Within these three are 26 metrics we use to measure the influences of those fundamentals, and most of these are widely published in the media. During this fundamentals section, I tried to provide as many free data resources as I could, however it's important to note that to unlock deep insights into fundamentals and indicators, InvestorKit spends upwards of $500,000 each year on our research division.

To break it down even more, these are my Top 3 must-know metrics out of the 26 fundamentals that you need to understand to successfully navigate the property market fundamentals at a macro level:

1. established supply for sale and rent

2. economic trends for a region of focus

3. local affordability.

Why these three? Without the property data terminology, these three points if trending well essentially mean this:

- there's not a lot of property for sale and not a lot of property for rent (shortage of supply)

- the local economy and job market is strong

- locals can afford property there, which will further support price growth.

It's hard to find a market where it's unlikely to perform well in the short term when those three points are all strong.

* * *

To recap on what we've covered so far, you have now read and unlearned the most common myths around the property market. Then, we looked at the property fundamentals to give you a strong foundation from which to base your decisions and action. Next, it's time to put them into action and get you thinking about how to apply your new knowledge. We're going to unlearn another well-known property tool, and replace it with our InvestorKit frameworks.

Grab Your Free Bonus Resources!

Enjoying the book? Head to
www.investorkit.com.au/book-resources
to unlock your exclusive bonus materials, tools, indicators and templates designed to help you take action and get results.

Don't miss out – they're free and ready for you now!

PART III

MARKET CATEGORISATION FRAMEWORKS

If part II was about going back to basics and building your knowledge of the property fundamentals, then part III is about starting to put all of this into action. Taking the key indicators and metrics that you now know, part III is about understanding how to apply your knowledge to ultimately better understand the way the market moves and behaves.

Guess what? It involves unlearning another popular property concept – which you'll know as the 'property clock'. In this part, I'll describe how it's impossible to apply the analogy of a clock to time market cycles perfectly and equally. Instead, I use market categorisation split into three distinct cycles – early-adopter, hotspot and second-wind – and explore why they're better than the property clock and why this is important for you. For example, different markets will suit different buyers, and it's got nothing to do with where the theoretical hands of a property clock lie.

I'll also introduce you to our spider charts, which I use to illustrate the market categorisations. These are a much more effective way to read the core drivers of a market and understand what's going on behind the scenes. Each market categorisation has its own spider chart, evolving the metrics you learnt in the previous part and helping you understand which are the most important to pay attention to.

Let's go!

Chapter 11

UNLEARNING THE PROPERTY CLOCK

I f you're anything like me when I started to get excited about property, you'll be familiar with what's called the 'property clock'. This is a commonly used method in the media to describe the so-called 'cycles' of the market through the analogy of a clock face. It's a supposed way to work out what city is in which stage, to rationalise the different phases that a market is in and what it's expected to do in the future so you can accurately 'predict' where to invest.

Typically, 12 o'clock represents the market peak and 6 o'clock represents the bottom. It's based on the commonly referenced phases of the property cycle – a 'boom' followed by a downswing in prices, a 'bust' as the market hits the bottom of the cycle, and then a recovery period as the market builds towards the next boom. These types of words are often used by the media, with everyone loving 'boom towns' as some sort of magic wand to time your investment success.

THE PROBLEMS WITH THE PROPERTY CLOCK

Firstly, I began to realise that I was getting confused by all the clocks out there. One minute, I was excited about an area because it was at four and about to go to six, and I was seeing this perfect circle. Then, suddenly, the four on someone's clock was now a nine on a different clock, and it felt like I missed the bottom. Or I saw an area at 9 o'clock and thought, great, that's now doing well. Someone moved it to 12 on *their* clock, and now I was worried about investing in it because I thought it might be at its peak, and I had missed out. I was looking at all these clocks ticking and growing anxious, thinking that everything was moving around so much. Surely, markets couldn't be changing that quickly or moving in so many different directions, could they?

Secondly, the property clock is a tool describing market cycles commonly used in Australia because it's so easily understood by many. As I mentioned, it goes through from the declining times of one to three, then three to six, where the market is near its bottom, then six to nine, recovering, and finally nine to 12, representing a rising market gaining lots of strength before it reaches a peak. But because of the way the clock is designed, it appears as though each increment from twelve to one and one to two to three – and so on – is an equal amount of time. Of course, they're not; the market doesn't move in neat increments.

WHAT DOES THE DATA SHOW?

Let's see a market in real life and apply the property clock concept: Sydney from 2012 to 2017. During this time, Sydney saw a huge boom comprising five years of massive growth. Let's say in 2012, the market was somewhere between six and nine o'clock; then, in 2013 and 2014, it rocketed with capital growth increases. Many put its value at the peak – 12 o'clock – and said that it'd boomed for two years and that Sydney's at a new peak rising rapidly and couldn't keep rising.

Greater Sydney House Price Trend vs Annual Growth Rates
2012–2017

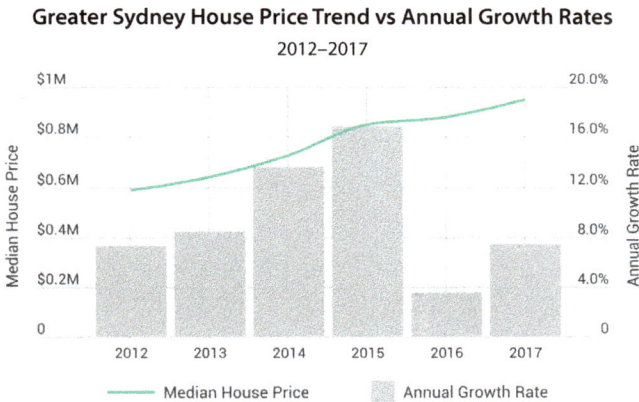

Source: Domain Insight | Prepared by InvestorKit

But then Sydney grew even more for another three years. If you had listened to the noise and avoided investing, you would've missed three years of double-digit growth percentages every single year simply because you put it at the peak level from 2013 to 2014 in a hot market.

The same thing happened in 2022 in regional markets like Toowoomba, Bundaberg and another major capital city Adelaide. Each experienced two years of booming results and everyone assumed they couldn't keep booming. But guess what? They kept booming for another two years with some more growth expected!

Median House Price Trends in Toowoomba, Bundaberg and Greater Adelaide

2020–2024

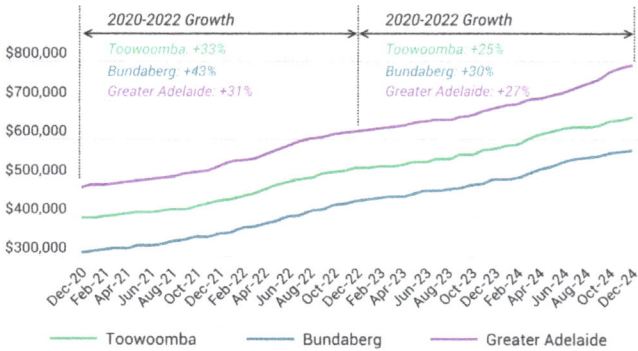

Source: Domain Insight | Prepared by InvestorKit

Now, if we come back to Sydney in 2017, the market finally started to decline. You might think if it'd spent five years booming, maybe it was going to keep going for another five years. But suddenly, two and three years went by, and by the end of 2019, Sydney stopped falling and fell flat for 2019 and 2020.

Greater Sydney House Price Trend vs Annual Growth Rates

2012–2022

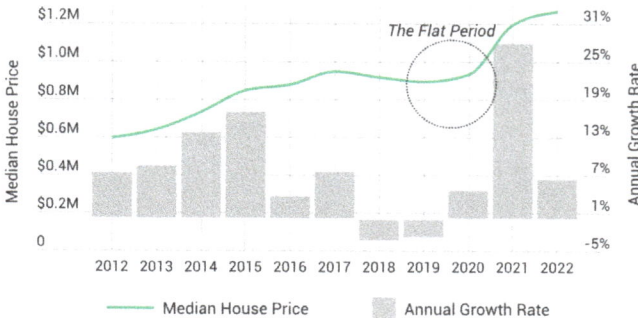

Source: Domain Insight | Prepared by InvestorKit

You've got to move your dial from one or two to three to six at the bottom, quickly. Then, Sydney started rising again in 2021 and your dial moved to nine and kept rising. Then, interest rates started increasing in 2022 and you had to move the dial from nine to three because it was declining again.

Greater Sydney House Price Monthly Trend vs RBA Cash Rates

Jan 2022–Dec 2022

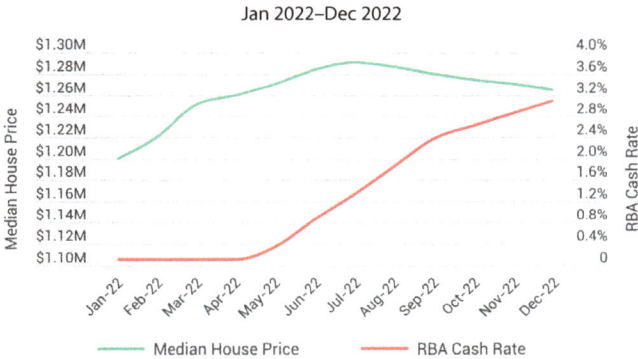

Source: Domain Insight; RBA | Prepared by InvestorKit

So, you can see that the clock is not a perfectly round, evenly spaced time sequence. And it tricks people into thinking a market is at 12 and that you shouldn't buy into the peak. The impact is that you could miss out on many years of growth simply because you believe in an imaginary concept. The clock keeps switching positions anyway, and you end up growing more confused, as per the Sydney example.

You can rarely find consistent market cycles let alone predict a market's trend merely based on its current position in a cycle. It's more like a mini-forecast of a place in a moment in time, and an overly simplistic way to 'understand' how the market moves.

This oversimplification echoes other asset classes, such as shares, with the common catchcry of 'buy low, sell high', which is also an incorrect way to look at property. For example, if we move from Sydney and look at the Brisbane and Adelaide markets, both performed weakly between 2012 and 2019. If we apply the buy low, sell high theory here, you might think that both Brisbane and Adelaide were looking affordable in about 2015 and buy something because you negotiated a cracking deal. You look at the clock, which positions both markets at the bottom and indicates it's a good time to enter the market. But then, nothing happens until the market finally starts to move again – five years later – by which time you've held a property going nowhere.

Median House Price Trends in Greater Brisbane and Greater Adelaide
2012–2020

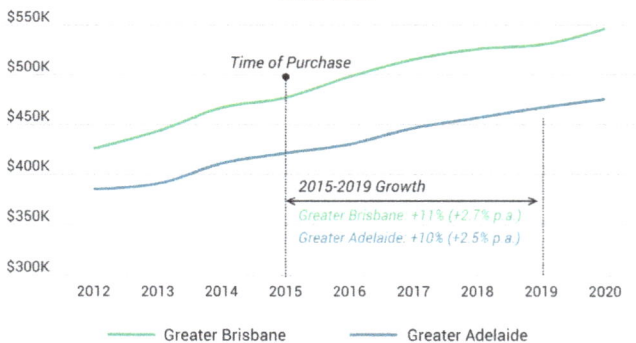

Source: Domain Insight | Prepared by InvestorKit

The same thing happened in Perth following the mining boom from 2008 to 2013. The market starts contracting, and you buy in 2017, thinking that the market can't keep declining and you're getting a deal much cheaper than anywhere else in Australia. But again, Perth keeps declining for another three years, and while you've bought low, it's not going anywhere, and you've missed out on years of good growth elsewhere.

Median House Price Trends in Greater Perth
2011–2020

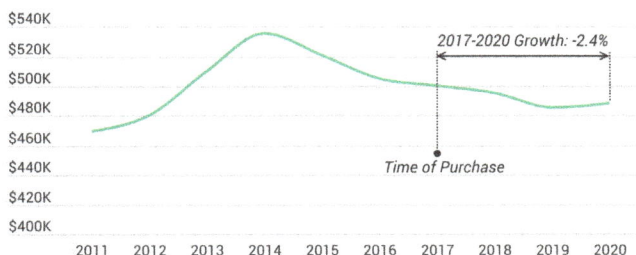

Source: Domain Insight | Prepared by InvestorKit

These two tables show the growth you could have achieved if you purchased elsewhere other than Brisbane or Adelaide (the first table) or Perth (the second table).

5 SA3 Regions Where House Prices Surged in 2015–2020

Region Name	Greater Region	2015 Median House Price	2015 - 2020 Growth
Sunbury	Greater Melbourne	$360,000	+58% (+10% p.a.)
Shoalhaven	Regional NSW	$380,000	+53% (+9% p.a.)
Casey - South	Greater Melbourne	$390,000	+51% (+9% p.a.)
Hobart - South and West	Greater Hobart	$385,000	+52% (+9% p.a.)
Geelong	Regional VIC	$380,000	+50% (+8% p.a.)
Benchmark: Greater Brisbane		*$476,000*	*+14% (+3% p.a.)*
Benchmark: Greater Adelaide		*$421,000*	*+13% (+2% p.a.)*

Source: Domain Insight | Prepared by InvestorKit

5 SA 3 Regions Where House Prices Surged in 2017–2020

Region Name	Greater Region	2017 Median House Price	2017 - 2020 Growth
Hobart - North West	Greater Hobart	$305,000	+36% (+11% p.a.)
Devonport	Regional TAS	$250,000	+32% (+10% p.a.)
Ballarat	Regional VIC	$332,000	+30% (+9% p.a.)
Launceston	Regional TAS	$290,000	+28% (+9% p.a.)
Orange	Regional NSW	$360,000	+25% (+8% p.a.)
Benchmark: Greater Perth		*$500,000*	*-2.4% (-0.8% p.a.)*

Source: Domain Insight | Prepared by InvestorKit

Finally, housing growth doesn't stop overnight just because someone thinks it has increased too much. It cannot replace people's rapidly changing sentiments; where individuals may suddenly not want shelter or a roof over their heads, or they may suddenly hesitate to enter the market and buy property, even when the economy and job market are strong, simply because they feel housing has risen significantly. They want to live in that city and be a part of it, and this situation can't be oversimplified into neat phases.

As an investor, there are pros and cons for every cycle and not every stage is everything it's cracked up to be. For example, if you want to be in a hotspot and gain great short-term capital growth, that sounds great. But be prepared to have little choice of stock, high competition and an agent who doesn't care about you because they know they have many other buyers they can squeeze for more money.

Also, consider your own portfolio and what it needs. Do you want to spend the next 12 months smashing your goals with fast growth in a hotspot market, or do you want to buy well, negotiate heavily and have a longer-term cycle ahead of you? The danger of only thinking of property in these terms is that it can cost you if you end up investing somewhere without understanding the bigger picture. It happened to me, and it can happen to you too!

With all of this in mind, I could see that the data wasn't representing these market movements. It's irrelevant. There are too many moving parts. Also, there's the bigger picture of being realistic about your personal goals and then looking at the pros and cons of investing in different cities. My team and I have observed so much noise and chatter from our forums and podcast questions around timing the market that I thought there had to be a better way to understand how the property markets move and behave and what markets do at different phases.

THE NEW WAY: MARKET CATEGORISATION

A few years ago, that moment hit me. There was a better way, and it had nothing to do with telling the time. Instead, let me teach you about the correct way of analysing markets through what I call 'market categorisation'.

In categorising markets, we look at a location's position in its market cycle and, more importantly, examine the local economic activity and demand versus supply trends in the form of market pressure to estimate market trends over the next year or so.

Market categorisation clearly explains where markets are and how you can find markets and properties in certain cycles just by looking at particular trends over the short term and longer term, as well as their current data points.

To understand this better, I've created three market categories that I use in my business to buy for our clients based on their specific needs. These are:

- early-adopter

- hotspot

- second-wind.

I'm going to introduce you to these three market categories over the next three chapters, so you can see how they work and why they're a more holistic approach for the property market. I'll also take you through a different visualisation: our spider charts. Not the creepy crawlies though – I've created three charts that illustrate how the market categorisations work.

If you can replace your thinking with these three and banish the image of the property clock from your mind, you'll start to see property in a whole new light.

How it works

The main thing to remember is that data moves slowly. It's not about someone deciding that a city has entered a new cycle or everyone choosing to list their property all on one weekend, leading to a sudden spike in listings. It's not like the stock market, which sees overnight changes; it involves analysing multiple metrics and observing a change with sufficient statistical reliability over time that indicates a shift in the market. This is where we come in. For example, when we can see that one year is starting to look much better than the many years prior, we can start to have more confidence as the data gets deeper and predict a new cycle is emerging.

In an 'early-adopter' market, this is exactly what happens. Over an extended period of time, something is changing, but because it hasn't grown for some time, it's got some catching up to do. We trust that change will lead back to its long-term growth rates of median price. It's an opportunity to enter a housing market before the masses and before too much steam has been let out.

If we look back at Sydney at the decade to 2012, it was at a weak point. From around 2005, there wasn't a lot of great performance. During that time, changes in the indicators started to show something new was growing. An early-adopter phase is essentially buying just as market cycles are starting to shift; it's in your favour and it hasn't done so well in recent times.

In an early-adopter cycle, you're getting in early and you're starting to see the market play out. The pros are that you won't miss out on anything; there are good buying conditions, less competition, and you're getting in the full length of the cycle. But the con is that you must be patient – the indicators are changing, and this can at times take place slowly over a couple of years.

3 Market Indicators' Trends in the Greater Sydney House Market
2010–2014

Days on Market:

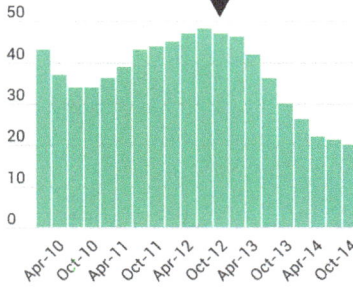

Vendor Discount:

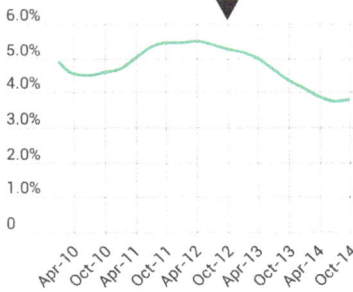

Number of For-Sale Listings:

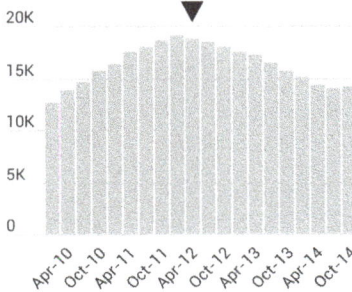

Source: Domain Insight; SQM Research | Prepared by InvestorKit

Let's look at Brisbane and Adelaide in a 'hotspot' cycle. In 2021, both are rocketing away. Their annual growth rates in all the data points are multiple times stronger than the long-term averages by a mile. As a result, they're no longer early but in a fast-growth cycle, producing high capital growth rates – they're a clear 'hotspot'.

Greater Brisbane and Greater Adelaide House Price Trend vs Annual Growth Rates

2014–2024

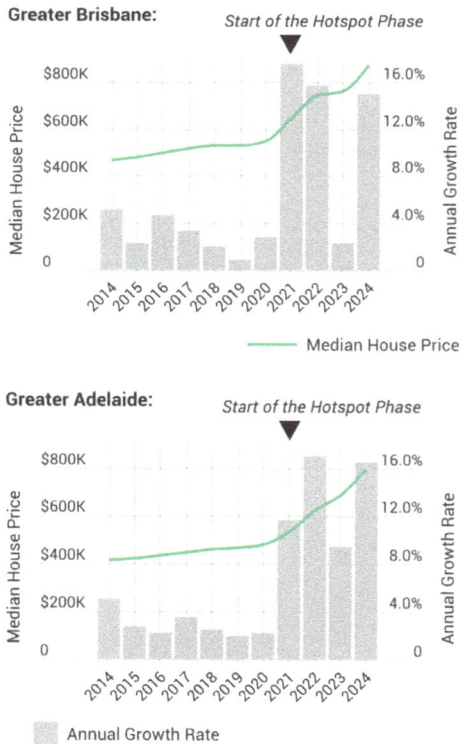

Source: Domain Insight | Prepared by InvestorKit

If there's an imbalance in demand, supply and confidence, a market will grow. It doesn't matter if that's six months, twenty months, three years or five years, if the imbalance is there, it's going to grow.

And the more growth, the more the imbalance will start to taper off, because it self-regulates if people can't afford it or don't want to invest in it.

That's the key to a hotspot. It's competitive. It doesn't fizzle, and it's where you'll get the highest growth rates. But the downside is it's hard to get in. It's very competitive, it's easier to make mistakes, and the longer and longer you leave it, the less growth you'll have because its demand and supply will eventually self-regulate.

We assess trends daily on the ground and at a data level to check if the imbalance is still there. If we find that it's far lower than it was when it first started to show, continues to taper off and then starts getting closer and closer to the end of this cycle, it could do two things. At this point, it flattens out for some time or it moves to the third market cycle: the 'second-wind'.

A second-wind market cycle represents a city that has gone through a boom, and is taking a breather before another run is anticipated. Examples of this are Sydney booming between 2012 and 2017, rising 66.8%, and then declining between 2017 and 2020 before booming again in 2021 and parts of 2022.

Greater Sydney Median House Price Trend by Month

Jan 2012–Dec 2022

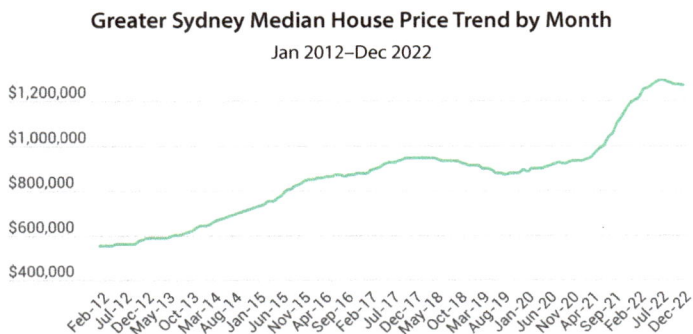

Source: Domain Insight | Prepared by InvestorKit

Another example is Brisbane in late 2022. The city took a small breather during its boom, listings increased and local conditions calmed down, before it had another surge.

Greater Brisbane Median House Price Trend vs Number of For-Sale Listings

Jun 2021–Jun 2024

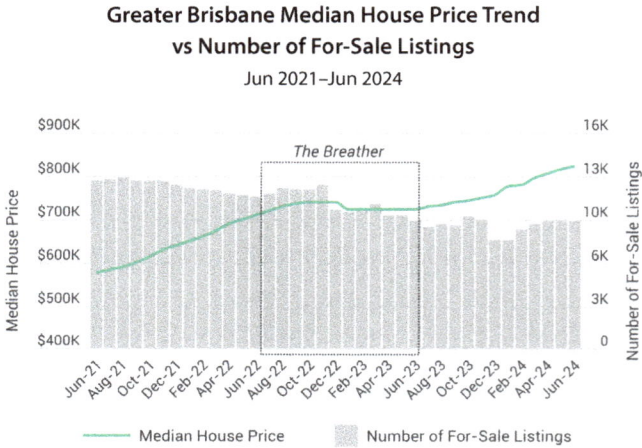

Source: Domain Insight | Prepared by InvestorKit

There are various reasons why these markets return or even take a breather. In Brisbane, it was a surge in listings close to when interest rates started rising that created that first phase of weakness and in turn a buying window. In Sydney, it was a combination of factors: an oversupply from the previous boom, lending, foreign transactions scrutiny and investment policy changes, negative gearing scares, and affordability shifts self-regulating the city.

As restored confidence returned in these markets they both recovered quickly, bringing the second-wind to life.

Often the most challenging for second-wind markets is predicting whether that buying opportunity remains for too long creating stagnation, or if the fast price growth phase part of its cycle ends quickly considering the city has boomed in the past.

That's why it's important to look at a city's fundamentals, as you've now learned. It was clear that the momentary pause in

Brisbane was a clear shift in seller and buyer attitude during the first wave of interest rate increases. However, as the local market adjusted and people realised things weren't as bad as they thought, it resumed its boom almost immediately, with listings reducing again as demand outweighed supply.

All market cycles have two phases. One, where they're just picking up market heat in their respective cycle, and two, when they're coming to the end of that cycle.

Market Categorisation Cycle Curve (Indicative)

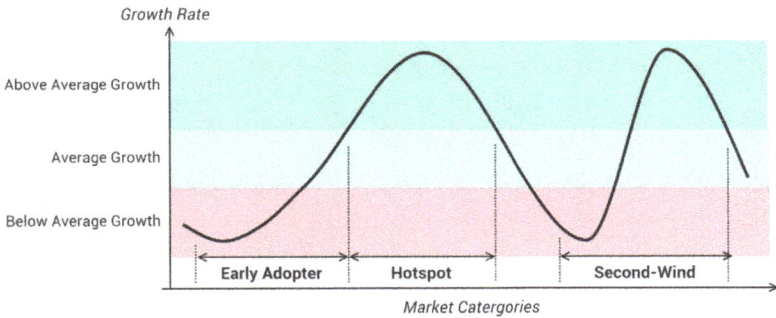

Source: InvestorKit | Prepared by InvestorKit

For an early-adopter, phase one is when trends start to initially show that were not present for the many years prior in that city, and then when they intensify they move towards becoming a hotspot (phase two). Hotspots have the highest rates of growth in their phase one, and then in phase two those markets achieve well above average growth but taper off from phase one. Second-wind markets in phase one are about a weak period of performance that represents an early-adopter-like entry point, while phase two is similar to hotspot markets. However, both phases in a second-wind market don't last as long.

THE NEW WAY: SPIDER CHARTS

Now that you have met the three market categorisations and, hopefully, moved on from the property clock, I want to share with you the next step, and a better way. I've created a stronger tool to visualise these cycles and how to look at the data to best understand which category they sit in: spider charts!

I created three spider charts a few years ago to illustrate a market holistically with its key indicators. Taking the analogy of a spider's web, it's a simple way to make something complex easy, taking the layers and spreadsheet columns and rows that don't make much sense when you're looking at hundreds of numbers and turning them into a clear and easy-to-understand chart.

Basically, each chart takes the same fundamentals and indicators that I've presented throughout the book and turns them into what resembles a spider web. Then we take the data of each indicator and rate it from one to five, which pulls in or out the line connecting each one. The more 'full' the chart or line with numbers pulled to around five, the better the market is performing and the more likely that market cycle is to grow. This is demonstrated by the following charts.

Indicative Spider Charts: High- and Low-Performing Markets

High-Performing Market:

Low-Performing Market:

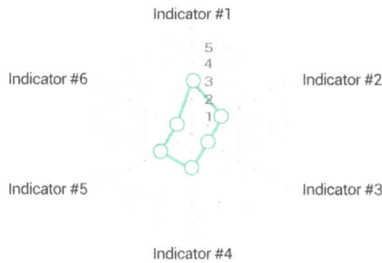

Indicator #1

Indicator #6

Indicator #2

Indicator #5

Indicator #3

Indicator #4

Source: InvestorKit | Prepared by InvestorKit

Now, not every city has a perfect spider chart and every city spider chart is unique. But the three I've created are the most typical to illustrate what's happening in the market for each of the three cycles, which is an easier way to understand what is happening and how you can apply the chart to different cities or places you've identified as places of interest.

Each chart includes the same following indicators:

1. *Economic activity:* Infrastructure pipeline and per capita spend, job advertisements and unemployment, local finance trends and spending data, airport passenger movement, population movements, gross regional/state product (GRP/GSP).

2. *Future supply:* Construction approvals in the pipeline as a proportion of established stock in the area.

3. *Established supply:* Listings for sale, their trends and trend intensity. Today and today vs last one, three, five, seven and ten years.

4. *Housing availability:* Listings for sale as a proportion of current houses in the area.

5. *Rental pressure:* Vacancy rates, rental price changes, rental yields and rental days on market.

6. *Price pressure:* Days on market, inventory levels, sales volumes, vendor discounting, auction clearance rates, asking and selling price changes, affordability, and forecasted price growth using machine learning and AI.

Over the next three chapters, I'll show you these three market cycle frameworks in more detail, as well as the spider charts that illustrate them.

Let's go!

Chapter 12

EARLY-ADOPTER MARKETS

The first phase of the property cycle is the 'early-adopter'. This is a market that has come out of the last cycle slump and is gathering market pressure for growth. It's not hot – yet – so you'll have less competition and a higher chance of getting a discount. If you think about this as the beginning of a market's expansion phase, it's a great way for investors to enter the market. Prices are usually cheaper and the competition is low.

RECOGNISING AN EARLY-ADOPTER MARKET

Taking into account the key indicators I've just outlined, the tell-tale signs to pay close attention to are:

- *Economic activity:* In an early-adopter market, the economy should be strong or recovering. A local economy plays a critical role in the recovery of a city. It also leads to a more sustainable growth cycle when it kicks off as local affordability and capacity remain strong.

- *Future supply:* This should be low, especially after many years of oversupply in a weak market. The prospect for success isn't high for builders in a weak market and so the future pipeline would have been reduced over time.

- *Established supply and housing availability:* This should be declining too but not by much, which you can identify using stock on market percentages and listings trends. In many early-adopter cycles these trends can be the last to change as the higher supply leads to less competition and better buying in this cycle. It's also these data points that need patience. Until the score for these two sections improves considerably, the market won't turn into a hotspot.

- *Rental pressure:* The rental pressure must be healthy as vacancy rates need to be low in an early-adopter market. The influence of the rental market is a common theme across the three markets, because this provides some solidarity and rental certainty to your portfolio. Healthy and rising rental markets while price pressure is weak creates an environment for increasing yields. Increasing yields attract investors, and increasing yields aren't attractive to tenants who may also more actively consider buying where possible. While you're waiting for the cycle to move into a hotspot phase you want to be able to comfortably secure rental income, which is why this is consistent for all phases and markets.

- *Price pressure:* In an early-adopter market, price pressure shouldn't score too highly otherwise it's closer to becoming a hot spot. However, it should be improving. Lower price pressure with all other trends starting to show signs of improvement offers property investors a great entry point into a market. Essentially, it's a future that looks promising but without the heavy competition (yet).

WHO IS IT IDEAL FOR?

Buying in an early-adopter market may not attract immediate high capital growth, but you will most likely enjoy an affordable purchase price relative to that market and be exposed to the whole growth phase in the coming years. The relatively low price allows healthy or higher rental yields than what the city has typically achieved in the past. Early-adopter markets are perfect for investors who can be patient and don't want the intensity of the competition to rush them, and will in turn benefit from the full cycle of growth when that time comes.

Active developers tend to stay away from early-adopter properties because they're not generally attracted to a slowly growing market. They prefer booming markets to grab short-term growth. Many do land bank in this market though if they can manage holding costs.

The early-adopter market offers full exposure to the market cycle – but you need patience. This one's about playing the long game. It's ideal for those who struggle with fast decision-making in hot markets. It's also for those who want to tick many personal boxes on an asset important to them in a lower competition market offering great prices.

THE EARLY-ADOPTER SPIDER CHART

The following chart is the spider chart for the early-adopter market cycle, displaying the scores to look out for. Remember the further a line is pulled out, the stronger its performance in that core indicator; for example, economic activity pulled out shows increasing strength in the economy (arrow up), and the future supply line pulled out is also strong (incoming supply is low – arrow down).

Early Adoptor Market Indicative Spider Chart

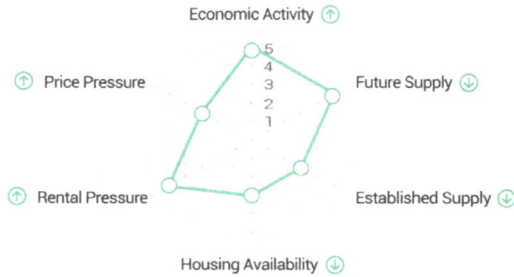

Source: InvestorKit | Prepared by InvestorKit

WHAT DOES THE DATA SHOW?

Our first example in this chapter is Perth from 2010 to 2020. I'm also going to show you Townsville from 2019 to 2020, so you can see how the early-adopter works.

You'll see I've prepared four charts that address annualised price growth, inventory, days on market and vacancy rate. I'll use the same four data metrics for each case study so it's easier to understand, rather than a mix of the different indicators.

In this first chart, across an annualised period of 10 years (one, three, five, seven and ten years) Perth's price growth had gone backwards. But in the last year, you can see that something was changing. It was only just positive, which to us suggests that the market was potentially about to take off. If you consider the spider chart, this is reflected by the 'economic activity' section.

Greater Perth Median House Price Annualised Growth
10 Years Back from 2020

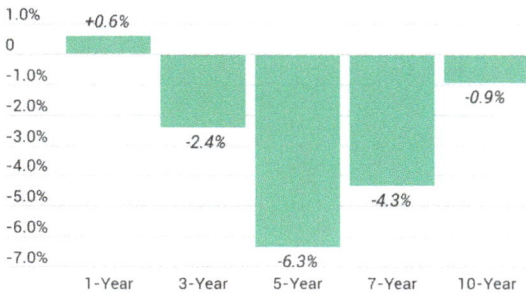

Note: 1-Year = 2019-2020; 3-Year = 2017-2020; 5-Year = 2015-2020;
7-Year = 2013-2020; 10-Year = 2010-2020;

Source: Domain Insight | Prepared by InvestorKit

Then, if you look at the second chart, you can see a trend where there are decreasing listings in this same period (2019–20). The number of listings started at around 22,000 and then slipped to 17,000, which in the spider chart is reflected in the housing availability and established supply.

However, the median house prices didn't change substantially, which you can see in the dark grey line, nor did the number of sales, which is fairly similar but creeping up ever so slightly. This indicates to us that more people are starting to buy, but there are fewer properties available and prices haven't risen – yet!

Greater Perth Median House vs Number of Listings and Sales Trends
2010–2020

Source: Domain Insight; SQM Research | Prepared by InvestorKit

In this next chart on the rental market for the same period, you can see rents started increasing in 2019 as the vacancy rate declined. It hit 2%, which is a high rental pressure benchmark, and kept travelling lower, yet the house prices hadn't changed.

Greater Perth Median House Rental Price and Rental Vacancy Rate Trends
2010–2020

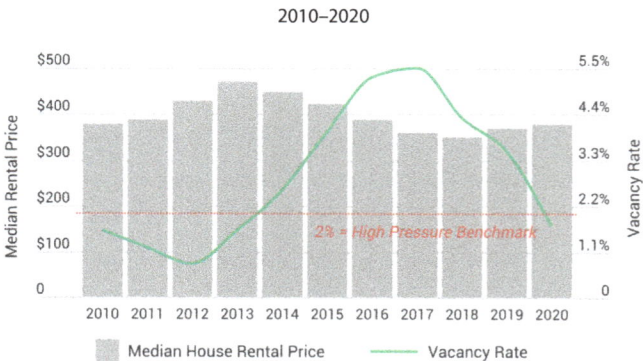

Source: SQM Research | Prepared by InvestorKit

Finally, the last chart shows the days on market and the house prices. Suddenly, the days on market began to fall. Properties were selling faster and becoming easier to sell too.

Greater Perth Sale Days on Market vs Median House Price Trends
2010–2020

Source: Domain Insight | Prepared by InvestorKit

Essentially, all four of these charts illustrate classic early-adopter trends, and we can predict what's going to happen before it happens. It was easier to find a tenant, there were fewer properties for sale and it was just the start of growth. As the cycle progressed from early-adopter to hotspot, the boom was in full force.

Greater Perth House Price Trend vs Annual Growth Rates
2010–2024

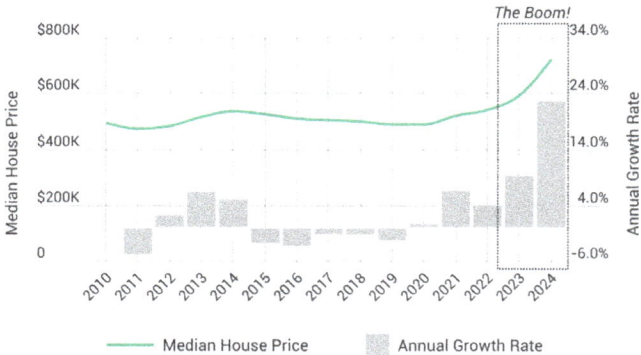

Source: Domain Insight | Prepared by InvestorKit

CASE STUDY

Nafiz Chowdhury – InvestorKit client

Nafiz began his journey as a property professional at 26. By the age of 30, he'd successfully grown his portfolio to three properties in three years. By making the most of our frameworks, particularly the early-adopter stage with his first property, he's now set up for life with nearly $3m in investment value and $1m in equity. Here's his story.

Before

Based in Sydney, Nafiz was living at home but keen to get his foot on the property ladder. His family shared what they knew – for him to access the first homeowner benefits and try to find an affordable apartment in his local area. As a young investor, this was also all he could afford despite the much lower prices in Sydney at that time, but this was his 'best' option with his lower income and lower savings.

The process

We advised Nafiz to buy a house, not a unit, and to ignore his family's wishes to limit his market options by buying something close by. Our suggestion was to buy an affordable house in an early-adopter market with a high yield, and we identified a suitable asset in Brisbane as the data was pointing to high growth ahead based on our algorithms – a classic early-adopter stage. We wanted to pinpoint high-growth markets before they boomed, despite the more obvious choices of affordable Melbourne and Sydney apartments with a solid track record of prior growth.

Nafiz went against his family's guidance, listened to us, and bought that Brisbane property sight unseen, far away from his home in Sydney. Had he listened to them and bought an apartment in West Sydney or the Inner West, it wouldn't have grown anywhere near what his Brisbane property did, giving him valuable equity and becoming his highest-performing asset. At the same time, he also focused on growing his career, increasing his earnings with each new position and allowing him to service more debt for more properties.

He then used the equity from his first home to fast-track the purchase of his second property in Sheidow Park, Adelaide. This was a classic hotspot property. We bought it in an extremely competitive market and aggressive campaign, where there were more than 50 people at the open home inspection. While this was a downside of the hotspot market phase at the time, the upside was that it resulted in high capital growth in just three years (62.6%), a phenomenal result for Nafiz. Remember, competition equals capital growth; without trends and activities that display competition, there's no hotspot present.

The third property was in Townsville, Queensland – another major market – reflecting our strategy of buying somewhere between an early-adopter and a hotspot and adding foundational assets in a major market while diversifying Nafiz's portfolio across the country. Our data indicated that this city had not seen growth for many years and was about to start a new boom.

Nafiz joined forces with his partner and bought his fourth property recently. At the time of writing this book, together with his partner, he has engaged InvestorKit for their fifth purchase.

The result

Each purchase has enabled Nafiz to fund the next property, taking advantage of early markets backed by data. He will have pinpointed high growth markets before they boom, and scaled his portfolio safely with diversity, different locations and affordability with well-placed yields, all tailored to the points Nafiz was at in his life at the time for each purchase.

After he buys all five properties, this will equal six years of investing to set him up for the rest of his life. He'll then focus on savings and earnings growth over the years ahead to eventually buy a home for him and his wife to live in. Nafiz remained a rentvestor through this whole journey, after moving out of home and demonstrating his sacrifice for his financial future.

Nafiz's property journey

- **Property 1:** Deagon, Brisbane, 2019 for $418,500
  Today's value: $820,000 (95.94%)

- **Property 2:** Sheidow Park, Adelaide, 2021 for $492,000
  Today's value: $800,000 (62.60%)

- **Property 3:** Kirwan, Queensland, 2022 for $445,000
  Today's value: $650,000 (46.07%)

- **Property 4:** East Bunbury, Western Australia, 2024
  for $595,000
  Today's value: $625,000 (purchased in November 2024)

Total portfolio value: $2.895 million
Equity growth: $944,500

Chapter 13

HOTSPOT MARKETS

Hotspots are the second in our three market cycles. The market is under high pressure in a hotspot and seeing accelerating value growth. The indicators are trending and currently hot, which is why you often see hotspot areas referenced in the media – they make excellent clickbait news stories!

RECOGNISING A HOTSPOT MARKET

In a hotspot market, the local economy is thriving and housing demand has been high for a while with very high confidence in the data, leading to high pressure in both rental and sales markets. Current supply levels are low due to the high demand, but you will notice in this spider chart new supply will increase soon. Developers are attracted to this hot market as it is easier for them to sell their product.

Buying in these markets, you could see your equity grow dramatically in just one to two years, but you'll need to be prepared for intense competition.

For this market, the indicators to pay close attention to are:

- *Economic activity:* Like early-adopter cycles, hotspots feature improving or thriving local economies, which is usually indicated by heavy infrastructure investment and low or lowering unemployment rates. A thriving economy assures increasing housing demand by boosting consumer confidence and attracting more residents.

- *Future supply:* A hotspot's incoming supply (new construction) level has been low for a considerable amount of time, leading to insufficient housing supply when demand surges, which pushes market pressure high. But the heat in the market can often trigger more construction activities, trying to take advantage of the robust growth phase. It's usual to see a surge in building approvals, a lead indicator of incoming supply. It's important to note though that increasing new supply doesn't weaken a market; rather it's a combination of increasing new supply and established supply trends together that make the biggest difference.

- *Housing availability and established supply:* The number of for-sale listings reflects established supply. Hotspots usually see a much lower number of for-sale than their pre-hot stage. Mistakes can be made in the pursuit of fast growth, or fear of missing out (FOMO) kicks in and people tend to buy properties in the frenzy that don't pass due diligence checks; for example, on a main road (more on this later). Low stock levels create this stressful behaviour, and it often comes back to bite.

- *Rental pressure:* Like early-adopter markets, hotspots feature tight rental markets and so high rental pressure. The leading indicator of rental market pressure is the rental vacancy rates – the lower, the tighter and the more pressure these areas are experiencing. Again, keep in mind that there needs to be high rental market pressure across all three market categorisations.

- *Price pressure:* While housing demand is lifted, the supply is not increasing as fast. Look at the gap between the total listings and total sales – if there are low inventory levels and fast-dropping days on market and vendor discounting, the metrics point to a hotspot. In larger markets, you will also see trending up and high auction clearance rates. It's near 63% to 65% in a balanced market, and not uncommon in hotspot cities for these to be between 70% and 80%.

WHO IS IT IDEAL FOR?

Hotspots feature tight supply, high demand, and attract intense competition. They are ideal if you seek high capital growth and are flexible on your budget, and are prepared to go for a great opportunity even if it's a bit pricier than you expected due to the moving target.

A hotspot is also great for first-time investors who have taken a lot of time to build a deposit and are trying to get their foot in the door. It may be beneficial to enter a hotspot for immediate, short-term capital growth over the next 12 to 24 months, leverage it, and then progress to the next property.

In short, a hotspot offers high confidence in short-term growth, but there is intense competition. Hang in there and don't take shortcuts. You'll need a flexible budget and to be seeking growth.

THE HOTSPOT SPIDER CHART

The next chart is the spider chart for the hotspot market cycle. Typically, the indicators rate a five, except for economic activity and future supply, suggesting that most of the market influencers are taking shape, trending and currently very hot. Economic activity isn't always a four; it can remain a five in some very strong local economies, it's just that most of the time a strong and fast-recovering economy spends most of its time in early-adopter mode as an early driver for the hotspot to come.

Hot spot Market Indicative Spider Chart

Source: InvestorKit | Prepared by InvestorKit

WHAT DOES THE DATA SHOW?

I've got a great example to share of Adelaide emerging as a hotspot over the two years from 2021 to 2022. It's worth mentioning that Adelaide's number of listings had already been falling over many years, as you can see from our first chart looking at the 10-year price vs days on the market, but I'm going to home in on these two years. Days on market is one of the indicators of price pressure, a key part of the spider chart. It's clear from the chart following that the fast-falling days on market is creating an increase in price pressure and in turn prices.

Greater Adelaide House Price vs Days on Market Trends
2012–2022

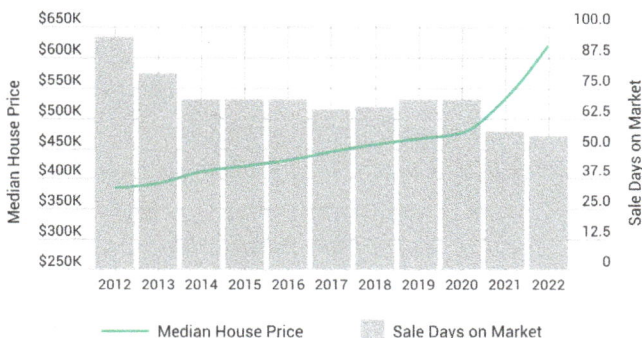

Source: Domain Insight | Prepared by InvestorKit

Price growth also needs to see upward movements as part of rapidly rising price pressure. In the hotspot phase, it isn't about hoping that prices go up; it's joining the wave of fast-rising prices, as evidenced in the next chart.

Greater Adelaide House Price Trend vs Annual Growth Rates
2012–2022

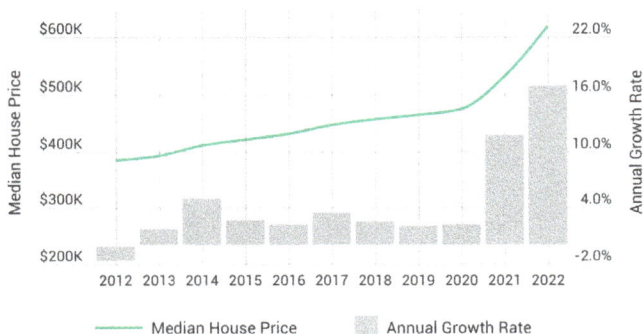

Source: Domain Insight | Prepared by InvestorKit

Continuing the focus on price pressure but now also housing availability and the established supply segments of the spider chart, it's apparent in the following chart that a hotspot trend is in motion. Listings are falling rapidly and sales activity is rising, indicating falling inventory levels.

Greater Adelaide Median House Price vs Number of Listings and Sales Trends

2012–2022

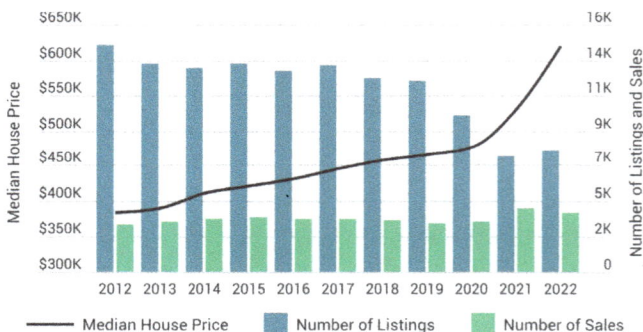

Source: Domain Insight; SQM Research | Prepared by InvestorKit

However, hotspot markets can't be hotspot markets forever, which is why it's important to look at the price pressure data contributing to the strong spider chart scores at very micro levels. When you observe things on the ground, you can identify trends and changes at open homes in relation to market pressure, for instance. You can assess based on days and weeks when on the ground, but the data on a chart will take a few months to appear. Together, both add confidence in the emerging trends.

Greater Adelaide House Price vs Days on Market Trends

Jan 2021–Dec2022

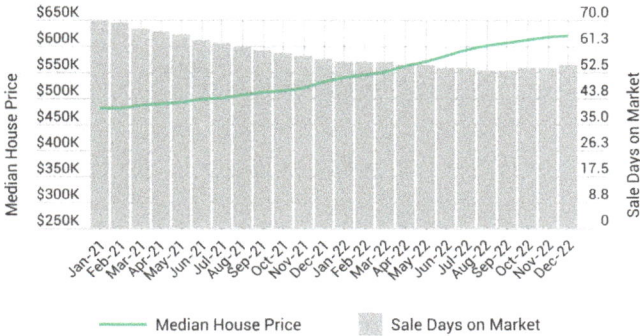

Source: Domain Insight | Prepared by InvestorKit

Greater Adelaide Median House Price vs Number of Listings and Sales Trends

Jan 2021–Dec 2022

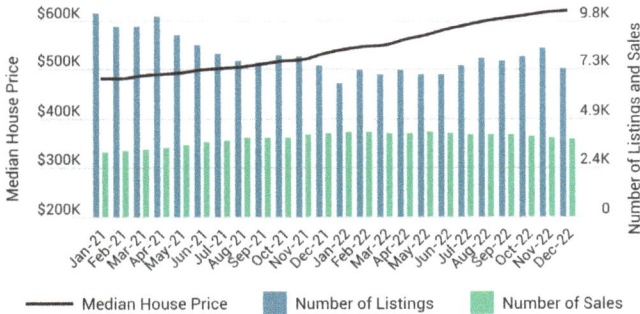

Source: Domain Insight; SQM Research | Prepared by InvestorKit

Similarly to the early-adopter market in Perth, a hotspot market in Adelaide or anywhere in the country, the market should have high rental pressure if you're considering making a purchase. The next chart shows the rental vacancy rates remained low and continued to decrease during the hotspot phase, while rents grew rapidly.

Greater Adelaide Median House Rental Price vs Rental Vacancy Rate Trends
Jan 2021–Dec 2022

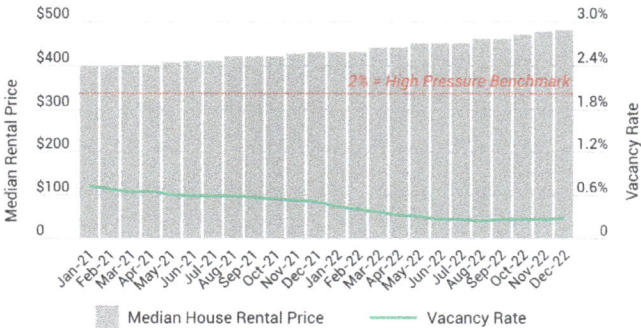

Source: Domain Insight | Prepared by InvestorKit

Hotspot phases can be the most exciting and nervous phase for an investor. When will it end? Am I missing out? Shall we increase our offer? Buy anything and don't worry about it to avoid missing out? Will we miss out again? All of these are common questions you'll ask yourself that bring both opportunity and risk. It's why many trust us to take the emotion out of the buying process.

CASE STUDY

Renjl and Bency – InvestorKit clients

Renjl and Bency are a couple with two kids in Canberra. They were accidental investors who transitioned from an underperforming townhouse into borderless investors with a portfolio of five properties, harnessing early-adopter cycles moving into clear hotspots. They now have significant property returns, equity growth of more than $820,000 and a great opportunity to achieve their dreams.

Before

Renjl works in IT, while Bency works in the medical field. They already owned their home in Canberra and an investment property prior to working with us and had become accidental investors because they upsized from a unit to a house and decided to keep the former. They thought they knew the market because it was their local area and that keeping the unit was a good way to build a portfolio, which they had decided to hold for several years.

Unfortunately, the unit didn't grow well but the house did. However, they had both become disengaged with the property process and for six years hadn't made any further investments. They didn't feel confident in their ability to fix their past mistakes and had developed a negative mindset.

The process

Our scaling strategy was to help Renjl and Bency get back to investing in a positive way with confidence. We advised them to consider regional markets far away from what they knew and access their home equity and savings to help their future purchase.

They trusted us, and we identified an affordable market early in its growth cycle, with a high rental yield in regional Victoria. At the time, Bendigo (where Epsom is based) was rising in value in 2018, and the trend started to show this was an early-adopter city and suburb. We went on to purchase the property with the couple trusting our process that regional properties grow, and as predicted, it continued to boom as a hotspot until 2021. It calmed down after that, but not before it created excellent growth.

After finding success and building trust with the first property, we went on to buy again in Adelaide in an area that was transitioning to a hotspot, and then again with their third purchase in Bundaberg, Queensland, which was also experiencing huge growth in 2021 as an emerging hotspot. With diverse properties across Victoria, South Australia, Queensland and their held properties in Canberra, we timed our entry into the Adelaide market before its boom, and then again in regional Queensland before its boom.

The results

Our clients were blown away that it wasn't just a fluke. We secured three properties in a row of high-performance assets for their portfolio, with equity growing a total of $820,000 not including their assets in ACT.

Today, Renji, Bency and their son and daughter are set for life thanks to generational wealth, which is important to them. With four investments and a home that can be downsized long-term as well as their superannuation, all of these come together and will compound over the decades ahead to achieve their passive income goals.

Renjl and Bency's next move will be a fourth purchase with us in due course either in their SMSF or a commercial asset down the track, something they're currently weighing up with us and their greater team.

Renjl and Bency's property journey

- **Property 1:** Epsom, regional Victoria, 2019 for $340,000
  Today's value: $600,000 (76.47%)

- **Property 2:** Ingle Farm, Adelaide, 2020 for $430,000
  Today's value: $740,000 (72.09%)

- **Property 3:** Avoca, regional Queensland, 2021
  for $425,000
  Today value: $675,000 (58.83%)

Total portfolio value today: $3.5 million+ including their own home and investment in ACT

Total equity growth: $820,000 (not considering purchases they made on their own)

Chapter 14

SECOND-WIND MARKETS

Second-winds are markets that have gone through a boom in the past five to ten years, are catching a second-wind and becoming a hotspot again. Second-wind markets come in two phases: phase one and phase two.

Phase one is akin to catching a falling knife. The market is declining and essentially moving backwards with a flattening of sales stock, so this carries some risk. You don't really want to be in phase one unless you can start seeing the flattening of the curve at the bottom, or the bottoming out of a declining market. Effectively, all of the weak trends flatten out.

At this point, there's a pro and a con. The pro is that if the market is coming around for a second growth cycle, you could be buying when everyone still doubts it. There could also be more stock, better negotiation and buy-in before others consider the downside. Of course, the downside is that the new cycle may not emerge and the market stays flat for some time with no signs of growing at all.

Phase two is the opposite: it's when the market starts to pick up again. We observed this in Brisbane in 2022, as noted earlier, when the market stabilised for approximately six to twelve months. However, a minor fluctuation led to an increase in listings, resulting in a strong growth rate for the market. It charged up again and was back in a growth cycle throughout 2024.

The pro of buying in a second-wind phase two is that because the growth cycle is active again, you'll see more growth similar to a hotspot. The con is that it usually follows a major growth cycle, so you can't expect it to keep doing everything it did in that first growth cycle for too long and you're in intense competition again. You're simply going into this phase to grab what's left in the tank.

RECOGNISING A SECOND-WIND MARKET

These markets offer good short-term value growth (like hotspots), but prices are usually not always affordable depending on the market, due to the previous boom.

In short, the second-wind offers a good diversity of housing stock. However, it presents lower yields in certain markets, as rental yields were suppressed from a previous boom, lack of affordability, and a limited growth cycle, depending on the intensity of the last boom. Recovering yields will occur, eventually catalysing the return of new investors in its second-wind phase – it's ideal for portfolio and opportunistic investors. For new investors, phase one of the second-wind phase is a buyers' market, allowing them to save for subsequent assets and diversify elsewhere.

For this market, the key indicators to pay close attention to are:

- *Economic activity:* Unlike an early-adopter or a hotspot, which typically feature a fast recovering or booming economy, the economic activity for a second-wind is usually relatively stable, or in some cases there may be some exciting economic activity brewing to bring on the second-wind.

- *New supply:* Unlike early-adopter and hotspot markets with low incoming supply levels, second-winds can often experience an increasing level of incoming supply. This is because its last booming period may have triggered more construction activities, although it would be tapering off in phase one. Phase two of the second-wind would again see more activity return in sub-regions within the city.

- *Housing availability and established supply:* Again, this is reflected in the number of for-sale listings. Second-winds usually see a slight increase in the number of listings (due to the end of the last boom) before decreasing again (entering the next boom).

- *Rental pressure:* To reiterate, there must be high rental market pressure for the second-wind market, just as there must be across all three market categorisations.

- *Price pressure:* Generally, second-wind supply can't cope with the demand surge. This leads to higher price pressure, although in phase one of a second-wind this will be relatively low. Many investors may wish to take advantage of this buyers' market.

WHO IS IT IDEAL FOR?

Second-wind markets are often reserved for two types of investors:

- If you're an experienced investor looking to diversify your portfolio further, and you already have exposure to various hotspot cities and states in your portfolio.

- If you're an investor looking to purchase in a market with a great negotiating opportunity and are looking to position yourself before the next rise.

However, you may not have the budget or appetite for the cities within a second-wind market. You may also have the patience to wait it out and be able to save to buy another property in another market cycle while this one brews away.

Second-winds are likely to be pricey with lower rental yields and limited growth, so they won't usually be your first choice if you emphasise higher cashflow or robust capital growth for a full cycle like an early-adopter buyer.

However, if you have built a sizable portfolio (with cashflow and capital growth secured) and are simply seeking diversity or great opportunities regardless of the price, second-winds can be ideal.

Second-winds can also suit first-time investors who are pre-pared to sit tight and wait – this one's about playing the long game!

THE SECOND-WIND SPIDER CHART

The following chart is a brief description of the market condition and trends. The local economy may not be as active as the previous two types, but it's still attractive, leading to high pressure in the rental market. Demand in the sales market is growing and stim-ulated by the second-wind, leading to lowering supply levels and increasing market pressure. As in hotspots, developers are active, so there could be a large wave of new supply on its way to relieve market pressure in the future.

Second-Wind Market Indicative Spider Chart

Source: InvestorKit | Prepared by InvestorKit

WHAT DOES THE DATA SHOW?

Many people think Brisbane boomed throughout 2020 to 2024. However, those not glued to the data (unlike my team!) would have missed a second-wind opportunity that occurred for a short window in Brisbane.

In the next chart, you'll notice a slowdown in the Brisbane market between August 2022 and December 2023. This was second-wind phase one, a buyers' market opportunity before Brisbane would turn from phase one to phase two of the second-wind, which surged in value.

Greater Brisbane House Price vs Days on Market Trends
Dec 2020–Dec 2024

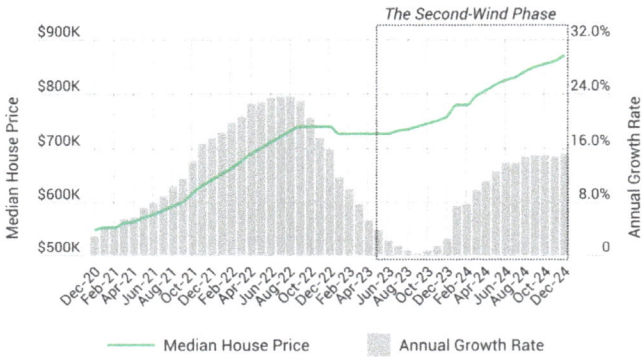

Source: Domain Insight | Prepared by InvestorKit

Listings trends increased during that time (mid to late 2022), while sales volumes were declining. This caused price declines, and then listings started to decline again, which brought the next wave of growth.

Greater Brisbane Median House Price vs Number of Listings and Sales Trends
10 Years Back from 2020

Source: Domain Insight | Prepared by InvestorKit

Rents continued to grow while prices remained flat for that short period, leading to an increase in rental yields. Rising rental yields attracted investors back into the market.

Greater Brisbane Median House Rental Price vs Rental Vacancy Rate Trends

Jun 2022–Dec 2024

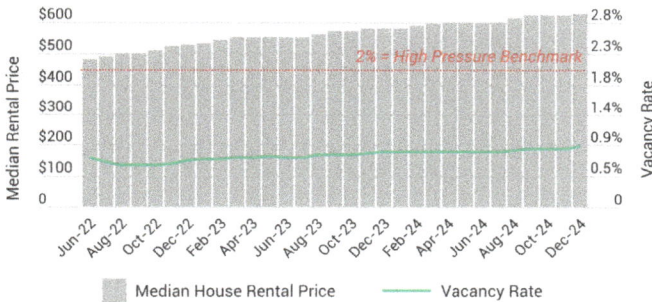

Source: Domain Insight | Prepared by InvestorKit

Days on the market also increased during the mid-to-late 2022 slowdown through to late 2023. However, after that increase period, it started to heat up again, and Brisbane returned to second-wind growth.

Greater Brisbane Sale Days on Market vs Median House Price Trends

Jun 2022–Dec 2024

Source: Domain Insight | Prepared by InvestorKit

While these are just some charts that showcase market pressure in Brisbane, they form key parts of the spider chart for a second-wind. They demonstrate how markets move in the categories highlighted, rather than around a perfect property clock.

When looking at all ends of the spider chart with a deep review of each of the influencers and indicators that make the cycle position of a city, you'll be able to achieve greater clarity on where and most importantly why you should or should not invest in a particular city.

CASE STUDY

Phill and Kerrl – InvestorKit clients

Phill is a land surveyor in a large engineering company, while Kerrl works in live television production at Channel 10. Based in Melbourne, the couple had a simple goal shared by many: to build a sustainable property portfolio that would support them in retirement. Build it they did, creating $520,500 in equity over four investments in three years, not including their PPOR (Principal Place of Residence). They took a steady and stable approach to their portfolio, choosing affordable properties with healthy yields spread across three states.

Before

The couple had bought an apartment in regional Queensland in their early 20s, which they worked hard to pay off. This gave them some security for their future, and then they moved to Melbourne and bought a family home in Brighton East, where they have remained.

The couple's plan had always been to buy one investment property every few years and hold them until they retired. But when they did the numbers, the calculator produced different figures every time.

They liked that we could pick markets and had confidence in the property market as a robust source of wealth building. Of course, we could see more potential for them than simply buying one property, and from day one, our recommendation was to buy somewhere interstate and go from there. Phill and Kerrl also understood taking out any emotion during their purchases. The properties had to be feasible as rentals and relatively low maintenance.

The process

Phill and Kerrl started their investment journey in 2021. They wanted to dip their toes in but weren't sure where to invest. Unlike many investors who simply use the broker attached to their bank, Phill and Kerrl engaged their own broker as well as looped in their accountant and financial planner.

We loved that when it came to buying their first apartment in regional Queensland, they jumped in early so that they could get onto the property ladder instead of waiting for perfect conditions to buy.

We helped them buy three more, including their family home in Brighton East, Melbourne. With each purchase, we worked together to make affordable purchases, securing loans within their means so they could live comfortably.

Central to our strategy was only buying affordable properties. While most were bought in hotspot market cycles, the second was purchased as a second-wind. In April 2022, the RBA raised interest rates, which was unexpected because they had previously reported they weren't going to increase them.

As a result, Brisbane experienced a minI slowdown. With the heat coming off the market, property listings dipped for the first time in about 10 years. Due to our experience in the Brisbane market, we knew it was a second-wind and that we had to act before everything rose again. We seized an opportunity in May in a suburb that was affordable for our couple, and we bought it for them.

Sure enough, the Brisbane market boomed in 2023, and today, the suburb of Goodna is unlikely to be as affordable again. They seized the opportunity at just the right time!

The result

The couple built $540,500 in equity over four investments in three years (not including their PPOR). They were all affordable purchases with healthy yields, spread across three states when considering their PPOR. With their investments, investing plan, superannuation and PPOR, they're on track for a healthy retirement.

Phil and Kerri's property journey

- **Property 1:** Newtown, Toowoomba, Queensland, 2021 for $377,500

  Today's value: $580,000 (53.64%)

- **Property 2:** Goodna, Brisbane, 2022 for $415,000

  Today's value: $615,000 (48.20%)

- **Property 3:** Berserker, Rockhampton, Queensland, 2023 for $425,000

  Today's value: $535,000 (25.88%)

- **Property 4:** Mount Gambier, South Australia, 2024 for $492,000

  Today's value: $520,000 (5.69%)

TL:DR 3 TIPS

I introduced you to the way we assess the property market – with spider charts rather than property clocks. They look like spider webs, and they're a powerful representation of the core property fundamentals applied to the three market categorisations we use in our business. The key learnings from part III are the three market categorisations:

1. early-adopter
2. hotspot
3. second-wind.

In part II, I showed you our Top 3 must-know metrics, which apply to our three market categorisations. These are the only three things you need to know to be able to assess where the market is currently, where it's been and where it's headed – so you can make the most of market conditions for your own portfolio.

* * *

You've now unlearnt the myths, learnt the right property fundamentals, and then applied them to our three market categorisations.

This brings us to our next step: acquisition and due diligence. It's great understanding how to pick the market, but how do you buy well, and buy something that won't come back to bite you in the future?

Before we jump in, I want to take a step back. There are many indicators that go into reading market fundamentals and cycles. Earlier in this section on market cycles, I broke these down: economic activity, housing availability, established supply, future supply, price pressure and rental pressure, and their sub-indicators.

At InvestorKit, we compile fundamentals and market cycle analysis together using an approach called Macro – Micro – On The Ground research. We work through influencers, indicators and the categorisation of markets as explained in this book to pinpoint cities to invest in for our clients.

To take that analysis one step further, you must ensure you have the skill and expertise to review the indicators in the right way and to the depth needed. I cover what we do and our battle-tested methodology in the next part. By embracing technology and AI to build $1 billion+ of real estate experience, our methodology is also available to you in this guide:

https://www.investorkit.com.au/report/
investorkit-research-process.

Grab Your Free Bonus Resources!

Enjoying the book? Head to
www.investorkit.com.au/book-resources
to unlock your exclusive bonus materials, tools, indicators and templates designed to help you take action and get results.

Don't miss out – they're free and ready for you now!

PART IV
ACQUISITION AND DUE DILIGENCE

If you've made it this far – congratulations! You have now unlearnt the most common property myths, replaced them with solid fundamentals and put them in action with our 26 indicators, learnt three market categorisation frameworks using spider charts, and have even been able to understand all the indicators and ways to look at indicators through the InvestorKit research process. Phew!

Part IV is about acquiring your investment property, and how to make the best decision to buy using due diligence. Because it's all well and good to have the knowledge and a better grip on how the market is driven, but how about putting yourself in the driver's seat and taking action when it comes to the property itself?

In this part, I'll take you there. Due diligence is a big part of property success, and I'll step you through why this is so important and how you can avoid the dangers of a bad investment.

Don't forget, I invest for the long game, and I want to ensure that the property decisions you make today will serve you well over the future.

Let's go!

Chapter 15

UNDERSTANDING THE RESEARCH

The next part of your journey is possibly the most exciting – it's where you bring all your knowledge into one place.

But before we do that, there's one more area I'd like to cover first, and this will help bridge the gap between the frameworks and due diligence of the book. It's this: how we make up the spider charts. I want to share a little about our research process so that you can see the insight behind the frameworks, trust what you're reading, and ultimately have confidence in the charts.

The spider charts are created from a bunch of core and micro-data indicators put together, which we call 'groups'. For example, price pressure (which is one of the spider chart inputs) is made up of multiple micro-data indicators: inventory (sales and listings), days on market, auction clearance rates and vendor discounting. These groups sit alongside the larger indicators on the spider chart, such as housing availability and economic activity.

When it comes to the indicators themselves, and how we apply them to the spider charts, we consider them in three ways. Firstly, we examine their trends, whether they are rising or falling, by comparing them to past periods, such as the trends from the last 12 months, as well as those from three, five, seven and ten years ago, and even further back. Then, where they are now, which is about a snapshot view. And finally, relativity: how do they relate to other cities of a similar size, for example? Or to the population? We interrogate the figures to get a strong sense of what's happening in a particular market.

We also consider a bunch of other indicators, going even deeper than the spider chart indicators to determine the strongest market opportunities. We look at things like infrastructure spend per capita, media announcements and sentiment, banking policies, relative affordability, how prices are moving in areas, and the price segmentation of sales.

In summary, the fundamentals are essentially influencers, while the market indicators comprise the makeup of the spider charts. The influencers are assessed by the indicators to create the market categorisations, all working together to create the big picture.

EMBRACING TECHNOLOGY

It's great to access the data and look at the right numbers, but it's what you do next that makes the difference between an average result and an excellent one. You need to be able to interpret that data. For that to happen, you need the right team in place who have the skills and experience to read the information. At InvestorKit, we apply a rich mix of battle-tested methodology, technology and our own experience to interpret the data, and we have also embraced AI to be able to source, collate and research more data than ever before.

For example, we use AI to do back-testing to understand which indicators are more important than others. We have created our own models and weighted scoring systems to do some of this heavy lifting. These enable us to constantly monitor the data and, as a result, make fewer mistakes. We also deep-dive into a high-frequency market pressure review, keeping our fingers and toes constantly on the pulse.

Our team embraces technology by engaging the best and brightest data scientists and research analysts, and we are committed to exploring how the latest developments in AI can help us. We're not stuck behind spreadsheets but use forecast models to dig into the past and look to the future. We also apply a mix of charts and layered research platforms so we cover all bases. With more than 75 investment properties owned by our team, we certainly walk the talk, too!

Our aim is not necessarily to let you run wild in the investment market, but to empower you with the right data, the right information and the right people so you can get ahead and make better decisions over time.

Now, let's get moving!

Chapter 16

THE DANGERS OF GETTING THIS WRONG

I f you've carried out your research, assembled your team and are ready to buy, it's an exciting time. But like anything, there are dangers. At InvestorKit, we ensure that every property we look at is rigorously assessed against our due diligence checklist before we even think about acquiring it for our clients.

WHY WE DO DUE DILIGENCE

I can't stress enough how important it is to take the time to do your own due diligence. This involves thoroughly assessing the property's physical condition and local context, looking at comparable analysis, and, finally, considering your own cashflow analysis and portfolio fit.

We'll get into the specifics of these steps later, but for now, let's consider *why* we do due diligence. In my experience, it comes down to three reasons:

1. to reduce unforeseen costs
2. to reduce the impact of a property's future sales price
3. to ensure the property can be easily tenanted.

Generally, if something takes longer to sell, this usually impacts the sales price. Added to that are issues with finding a tenant for the property, which can blow out your holding costs. Unless you've tested these in your due diligence, you may face unexpected costs that can affect your portfolio and cashflow.

For example, let's say you find a place and fall in love with it because it's north-facing, and you've read that everyone loves properties that have lots of natural sunlight. The fact is that this might not be what actually makes a difference in selling the property – it's just a 'nice to have'. A north-facing orientation doesn't mean that a property sells faster, is easier to tenant, has no maintenance issues or a price difference compared with other nearby properties. You need to test it and start applying more rigorous data!

All or nothing

When it comes to carrying out due diligence, I find generally that people fall into one of two categories. They either don't do it at all, or they go overboard and have a list of 50 items to tick off.

Little or no due diligence

The greatest danger of not doing any due diligence is the surprise factor. You don't want anything to surprise you that's in your control because it will usually cost you money in the long term. Yes, things always pop up unexpectedly, but there's no excuse when it's an issue you had the ability to prevent in the first place.

To give you an example, I often see buyers celebrate a cheap purchase price. They think they purchased better because they did a quick comparable sales study, got a steal and got the deal done. But they bought on a main road, justifying it because it had four bedrooms and supposedly great rental potential.

Where they've gone wrong is that while the property was sold to them for a slightly better price, they'll have issues when they look to sell the same property in the future. The same discount they received will be compounded if someone else is also seeking a discount on the future value. They're not really saving anything.

There are other examples too, such as floods and bushfires. If you don't check that your potential property could be impacted by major floods, you might attract higher insurance costs for unforeseen events and a very stressful time if you need to make a claim.

The same thinking applies to the future sale of that property. Other people might do their due diligence and check for major flood or fire impacts or if it's on a main road, which means they could pass on your property and you'll take longer to sell it. You're not really saving anything in the long term, because the next buyer will expect the same discount you received.

Too much due diligence

You can have *too many* items on your checklist. Yes, you're exercising extreme caution by having 50 concerns to tick off, which is a positive. You're being conservative and considered, but the problem is you could be putting yourself in a position where you have to say no to too many deals because you can't tick everything off. You could risk passing on a decent investment if you see the data's right, but you still have some detractors on your list so you don't act.

You might feel as though you're doing the right thing by having such a thorough checklist, but you're shooting yourself in the foot. Remember that most buyers in the property market take between 6 and 12 months executing a purchase – waiting for so long and missing out on so many deals could be counterproductive to your growth strategy, especially in a hotspot market when each month can be over 1% of the purchase price in growth. That's $7,500 and growing per month on a $750,000 property – not a small figure at all!

Getting it right

You can avoid all of this with a clear due diligence process. With the right approach, you can make stronger and more informed portfolio decisions with less stress and additional costs.

As you'll learn next, we've created a process that takes in 20 points – not 50 – as a list you can apply when you think you've found a property worth buying. If your property makes it through the 20 points while avoiding serious risk factors, you'll be well placed to move forward, as long as it also works for you financially. (This list is provided in the next chapter.)

To create our list, we considered a series of key detractors and explored them in detail. For example, if we return to the example of buying on a main road, we check it against the variables. Did the main road impact the property attracting a tenant? How much discounting occurred on main roads in the area? Would this impact the time to sell? And would it also impact future sales or renting? Then we back-test these issues against the data and our market categorisations. That way we can see thousands of sales on main roads going back many years in hot, cool or flat markets. If there were many responses that were unfavourable for the buyer, this issue made the checklist.

ARJUN'S INSIGHT

As an investor, you must take the emotion out of the property process. Working through a checklist of points that have been carefully screened by experts should give you confidence that the main detractors of any property have been considered. It's easy to understand and simple to research further about the property if needed. Investing therefore takes on a different perspective through data and numbers!

Chapter 17

THE 20-POINT DUE DILIGENCE CHECKLIST

W hen it comes to searching for a property, it's easy to revert to what you think you know best. Hopefully, by now, you've learned that the old ways aren't necessarily the best ways. Instead, I'm going to share with you the checklist we use behind the scenes to provide you with a thorough and rigorous way to select the best property for your needs.

THE BIGGEST DETRACTORS WHEN LOOKING TO BUY A PROPERTY

Later, I'll show you our micro market analysis in which we explore comparable sales, cashflow analysis and portfolio fit. For now, here are the 20 points we've created that cause the biggest detractors when looking to buy a property:

The due diligence checklist

1. Highways
2. Cemeteries
3. Industrial areas

4. Major power lines
5. Energy substations
6. Swimming pools
7. Individual unit/villas
8. Land < 375sqm (pending area)
9. Extremely odd-shaped blocks
10. < Three bedrooms for a house
11. Multiple extremely small bedrooms
12. Train tracks and stations
13. Bus stops
14. Busy roads
15. Roundabout proximity
16. Directly facing schools
17. Flood-related impact including 'overland flow'
18. Bushfire risk
19. Major and unapproved alterations
20. Neighbourhood public housing commission rate > 20%

All of these points are carefully geared by us to give you extreme confidence and quality control so that you aren't going to overpay when you've found a property you think is worthy of buying.

They're also easy to assess yourself simply by reading the property listing, looking at its location map, or contacting the selling agent and asking them. For example, the listing won't mention if all alterations have been approved, so that's something to check. I've seen instances where outdoor areas – such as decks or even backyard dwellings – have not been approved, which means it has been illegally built and could be subject to removal.

The points above all have three key impacts:

1. sales price (down)
2. vendor discount (up)
3. time on market (up).

For example, if you find a property that's next to a highway, creating a lot of noise, that's a common detractor that encourages vendor discounting. A highway will also lift the time on market and so bring the sales price lower.

All of the detractors have the same effect – the trick is to ensure that the property you're considering passes all of the checklist items. Remember, I want you to find a property with high appeal and high resale value so you can create high streams of growth and income.

We created this list of detractors by looking at the hot and cold periods in any given market. Then, we looked at large sample sizes and conducted reviews of all these things in isolation and in grouped bunches. Finally, we examined these over extended periods, such as 5 to 10 years, to track resale transactions of both impacted and unimpacted properties across multiple cities, ranging from smaller cities with populations of 20,000 to 30,000 to larger cities with populations in the millions.

We found that when grouped into buckets, we could see these varying impacts. Yes, you can absolutely buy something cheaper than a comparable property, but understand that there's a future impact, and is it truly comparable if one passes your checklist and the other doesn't? The property value should still grow over the long term due to the land value, despite any detractors. However, the unknown suggests that it may be better to avoid purchasing it altogether, especially since true value growth is only tested upon resale.

MICRO MARKET ANALYSIS

This isn't a must for all investors, but it's something we do that you might find value in understanding. Basically, it's where we investigate specific suburbs before drilling down into the property specifics. We conduct field trips, and we do suburb filtration so that we can remove or consider suburbs with big data outliers, which we think will impact growth.

We continually stay in touch with the location by being well connected with local agents, property managers, building and pest inspectors, and brokers so that we understand what's happening on the ground, instead of waiting months for real data to show up on spreadsheets. We also visit the location personally too (if it's easy to get to), creating a full picture of whether we think it's going to be a good performer over time.

There are many property books that talk about understanding the local area and meeting the property experts who work in it, and while we agree, this is not always possible, especially if you aren't investing in your backyard without a professional team on your side (which is one of our property myths!). This can also be extremely time consuming, so you'll need to either start with the property or with the suburb and go from there, or have the right team around you already with those relationships.

COMPARABLE ANALYSIS

Once the suburb or property has passed your 20-point checklist, how do you know you're paying the right price for it? This is where comparable analysis comes in, which involves looking at the property's comparable sales and comparable rentals to establish its correct market value.

To do this, we use a five-point sliding rating scale similar to that which valuers use, which enables you to rate comparable sales as:

- superior
- slightly superior
- similar
- slightly inferior
- inferior.

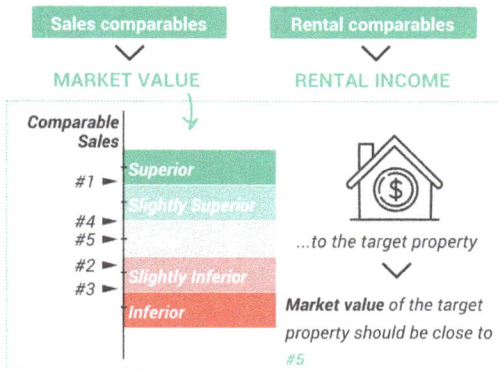

We apply these ratings to core factors taken from the due diligence checklist:

- land size

- interior and exterior of the property

- neighbourhood – which patch of the suburb it is in.

Then, we make adjustments according to the market heat and recency of sale.

This methodology aims to ensure you pay the right price for the property you're interested in and that it will make a good investment, based on solid data and information.

Often people will only look for 'similar' comparison properties. However, to increase confidence levels in your analysis it's important to consider properties that are both 'slightly superior' and 'slightly inferior'. You want to target properties that are slightly superior across the core factors. This creates a ceiling for what you should pay for that property, which should sit between the similar and the slightly superior, with the price floor above the slightly inferior or inferior ratings and near the similar.

For example, look for a property that's only slightly worse than the one you are considering, meaning that it's the closest possible to being as good as yours, but you can confidently say it's slightly worse because it has a flaw. If you look around and see that the best one you could find that's slightly worse sold for $1 million, you can tell yourself that there's no way you would buy for under a million.

It's not to say it can't happen – at the end of the day this is just a report you're creating for yourself – but this is an analysis to give you the balance between overpaying on a place and avoiding constant disappointment by regularly missing out as a market rises in front of you.

Now do the opposite: what's the worst property you can find that's slightly better than yours? Let's say the worst property that's slightly better sold for $1.15 million – so there's no way you're paying more than that.

This rating scale is a much easier way to nail your price because agreeing on whether something is worse or better is more effective than just saying that it's similar. It's like a sandwich: you have the top and bottom and a better measure of price in the middle.

ARJUN'S INSIGHT

Ensure you make adjustments that factor in market heat. For example, if the market growth rate is averaging 1%+ per month, a house that sold three months ago at $750,000 that you think is similar could be worth an estimated $772,500 today. In hot markets, this is a big reason why many people miss out. It's not that you got the comparable analysis wrong by selecting the right property, it's that you didn't take into account the heat in the market.

Sold dates aren't always the best to rely on because they can be marked differently from agent to agent. It's better to use the listing date if you have access to platforms like RP Data and CoreLogic. Often when a property is being sold, the most heat and activity in a non-auction environment is the first one to two weeks from listing. Utilising listing dates can help you avoid any days-on-market methodologies that vary from city to city and agent to agent.

CASHFLOW ANALYSIS AND PORTFOLIO FIT

The last step to acquisition is considering your financial situation and how the property will sit within your portfolio. There are whole books on this and I don't want to get into the nuts and bolts, but this is significant to your due diligence because everybody's cashflow and financial position is different, and this will affect the decisions you make as to the right time to invest.

Let's say you and I are first-time investors looking for a growth area, but our property requirements are different. You might be open to a larger purchase price and have larger savings with a bigger deposit or acquisition cost. I might need a minimum rental yield, because my bank said if I don't achieve $600 a week they won't give me a loan.

A cashflow analysis should consider the following:

- *Estimated purchase price:* Examined in this chapter.

- *Acquisition costs:* Stamp duty, professional services fees and bank fees.

- *Mortgage payments:* Often interest-only for investors, however this is your choice.

- *Holding costs:* Rates, water, insurance, property management, repairs estimates, vacancy estimates, land taxes and other compliance costs.

- *Capital growth:* 5% to 7% long-term averages.

- *Rental income:* Rent per week, multiplied by 52, divided by the purchase price and then expressed as a percentage equals rental yield %.

- *Rental growth:* 3% to 5% per annum long-term averages.

- *Inflation:* 2.5% to 3%+, mid to top end of RBA target bandwidth.

Remember that when you're starting out, most properties will follow your deposit trends. This is likely to be lower, while your debt may be higher. However, over time, as rental pressure mounts, your cashflow will improve as rents rise and circumstances begin to shift.

Finally, we use cashflow analysis to establish your portfolio fit. This is about how your portfolio aligns with your other life plans and goals. It's not just the property to consider but the bigger picture. Should you buy a property that's flashier and newer? Or are you comfortable with a property that might have a few dings that you could improve in the future? Should you buy a property and use up your whole million-dollar budget? Or go in for $600,000 to $700,000 because you're conservative and you need the space in your deposit? Or maybe you consider adjusting the state you're looking at buying in because you have four properties in Queensland, and do you really need a fifth one there? Maybe you could look at your current holdings and go elsewhere, such as to Western Australia or New South Wales instead.

* * *

A property might pass all these checks, and it might be a fair value, but if you aren't going to be able to sleep at night because of any of the reasons above, it might not be the best fit. And that's okay – you need to be honest with yourself and where you are in life. Consider everything: how you will manage repayments, your lifestyle, what the bank needs, and what you are comfortable with today and in the long term.

Chapter 18

THE GREY AREAS

I n this chapter, I want to point out that the 20-point checklist is specifically for investing. It's not for those seeking their primary residence, but for investors who are looking at facts and figures. You might already notice that there are some grey areas.

SWIMMING POOLS

Let me give you an example. As you'll see, a swimming pool is on the checklist. Swimming pools aren't necessarily deal breakers, but a swimming pool may have unwanted maintenance costs, and this will be part of the due diligence process you'll need to address. The swimming pool may also deter other investors who don't want to take on that maintenance. But you could always remove it and clear the space for a garden or landscaping.

Not all of our due diligence points negatively impact homes solely for resale; they may also involve additional maintenance considerations that could affect resale value. A swimming pool is one of these grey areas. Some markets perceive a pool as an asset; however, you must factor in the additional costs. None of my property investments include pools. My family home does, but none others.

LAND SIZE

Land size is another grey area. You can buy terraces in Inner West Sydney or terraces in Melbourne, and both can grow well in value despite being only 150 to 200 sqm. It doesn't mean that the smaller size is a bad purchase, but what we've done in our checklist is make the land size 375 sqm and higher – so that we have confidence from all types of buyers. We want all types of buyers to be reassured that any property considered as part of our due diligence will be 375 sqm or more.

However, if you lock in on an area like the inner suburbs of Sydney or Melbourne, for example, your analysis of comparable sales will be based on that. Smaller land parcels will make up a high proportion of sales in that area, and aren't new trends as in some outer suburbs, because they're already preferred and tested for decades. Hence, this also isn't a deal killer, pending the area in question.

ROADS

Roads are another anomaly. I remember going to a beautiful suburb in Bundaberg, Queensland, called Bargara, to see if I thought it would make a good investment opportunity, especially with its strong data points. It's a beachside suburb and a beautiful spot. If I had decided based on the long stretch of main road and bus lanes along the beach marked yellow at 60km/h, I would have immediately discounted it, because according to our detractor list this was a due diligence *no*.

But when I drove down this road, it wasn't busy at all! I saw five cars driving along it, more people walking and generally what looked like a beautiful town. Funnily enough, the road had attracted premium property sales. There were $3 million and $4 million sales in the suburb on this very street, which told me that this area offered excellent potential to continue with my due diligence, all because I did a field trip and saw it for myself rather than relying on Google Maps.

If I continue with the road analogy, another detractor is a road with a school on it. School zones are noisy and hectic at drop-off and pick-up times. So, as investors we may avoid a road with a school on it. However, not all roads go one way; they have two directions. Instead of coming out of your driveway and heading for the direction of the school, you can turn the other way, avoid the chaos altogether and go wherever you need to go.

An example is the suburb Trott Park in the south of Adelaide. It's an area on a hill between a highway on the left and a highway on the right. The due diligence alarm rings to avoid any suburb with a highway because it's noisy. But Trott Park has always had this configuration, and its pricing factors this accordingly; there are many houses towards the middle of the suburb that aren't right on the highways. As a result, it's performed well over the years. Upon closer inspection, we discovered that there were some areas with parts of their streets under a highway. However, if you avoid those areas and choose to be right in the middle, there's no issue as people are aware that the suburb is bordered by highways on every side. If it was a suburb that wasn't surrounded, one side of it would see the impact more than the other side, and mistakes could be made in comparable analysis (thinking you're getting a steal) when really you aren't.

FLOOD INTERPRETATION

Another grey area is flood interpretation. Some flood reports can look scarier than others and put you off as an investment opportunity. For example, in Townsville, Queensland, their flood reports apply a dark blue colour to highlight their lowest risk rating, and green, red and yellow to highlight the highest risk rating.

If you're looking at a property to buy there and you look on the map at the 'good streets' that don't flood, they can have patches of dark blue everywhere. You look at the flood report legend, which points to the smallest rating. This means that when water hits there, it only rises a little in that area. When you test this by looking at the insurance premiums, none of them are elevated in many of those patches, and in some parts, locals report no previous impacts even with the many major floods that have occurred. Lastly, looking at elevation levels and even resale or rent campaigns, these pockets had no negative impacts either.

Different maps do different things, and flooding reports aren't universally portrayed with the exact same details and interpretation by all councils, which can be confusing when you're looking at areas and their flooding potential. Clarify your understanding of area maps by speaking with councils and locals, or having a team that is well-informed about all these implications.

'ROUGH' AREAS

Finally, another grey area is 'rough' areas. These include what might be small zones of a suburb that are rougher, yet the perception is that the whole suburb is to be avoided. When you speak to a local, you might realise that one patch doesn't reflect the whole area, but you need that person on the ground to give you the real deal.

As I've mentioned, the best way around grey areas is to have professionals who are familiar with the market who can help. Obviously, it's impossible to visit every promising location yourself as an investor, but having someone in that part of the country who can give you an honest appraisal can make or break a property deal.

It's why we prefer public housing mapping tools, which you'll see reflected in point 20 of the checklist (the neighbourhood public housing commission rate). We have a comfortable percentage of the neighbourhood to consider as a cut-off (anything below 20%).

You can also conduct owner name searches of properties in the surrounding area to see which ones are large complexes of housing commissions. This means you could consider suburbs where the data is sound and not be persuaded by simplistic demographic comments or opinions that say 'it's rough'. You can instead focus on simply being in suburbs that present the best data, while avoiding the patches that impact resale or rental data.

PASSING DUE DILIGENCE, COMPARABLE ANALYSIS AND PORTFOLIO FIT

If you have applied all the elements in this chapter to a property you're interested in, and it passes, you're in an excellent position to move forward with it. The beauty of this process is that we've taken all the guesswork out of it – apply the detractors, and then see how it compares and how it fits with your goals.

Chapter 19

SUCCESS STORIES

What are the outcomes of good interpretation and data analysis and applying due diligence? Let's have a look at two more case studies of clients we've worked with to transform their portfolios with dramatic results.

LORNA WANG – INVESTORKIT CLIENT

Lorna is a great example of how applying due diligence has enabled her to scale her portfolio from one to four properties within three years, with equity growth of $1.1 million+. But she had to overcome a hurdle first. She'd done the right thing initially by making the jump and buying her first property, but she'd bought an apartment that was oversupplied in her backyard. Here's her story.

Before

Lorna wanted to grow her portfolio, but she was hesitant for a few reasons. Firstly, she'd lost confidence in her abilities. She'd bought one investment property in 2014 in Yagoona, New

South Wales, and it hadn't gone well. It cost her $367,000 and had shown no growth for five years. Even today, after 10 years, it's only shown minuscule growth.

But she was young, didn't have the income to afford a house in a growing area in the city she lived in, and she ended up choosing a small apartment in her backyard. Listening to her family and thinking it would make a great investment, she'd chosen an apartment with an oversupply in the area, so straight away it was always going to struggle.

The problem was that even though she was able to buy a second property while she had her first, because she had a strong income and great savings, she simply focused on paying it down and went into paralysis analysis.

Her other problem was that she hadn't applied due diligence to her search process. She'd trusted family members to guide her and believed that investing in a unit was the way to go.

The process

We turned it around for Lorna after meeting her via her mortgage broker. We built a strategy that involved harnessing the equity in her property that she'd paid down and some of its growth to purchase the next asset.

We targeted affordable properties – houses – in markets primed for high capital growth using data, with healthy rents to make it easy for her to hold them. From the outset, our plan was to apply a borderless strategy as well as diversify across multiple states for market performance, offering tax savings and access to both early-adopter and hotspot cycles.

From where she was mentally, Lorna let go and trusted us to help her and guide her through the process. We went on to purchase four properties for her in two years, using her income, high yields, tactful lending strategies and rapid price growth in her assets allowing her to roll up the equity into multiple assets.

The results

Lorna's portfolio has gone from an underperforming unit that only grew from $367,000 to $495,000 in 10 years, to a multi-million-dollar property portfolio with more than $3.14m across five assets in total spread across four states (Queensland, South Australia, Victoria and New South Wales). By using careful due diligence, Lorna's portfolio has generated a total equity growth of $1.289 million, representing life-changing results.

Lorna's property journey

- **Property 1:** Yagoona, New South Wales, 2014 for $367,000

  Today's value: $495,000 (34.88%)

- **Property 2:** Adelaide, South Australia, 2019 for $395,000

  Today's value: $745,000 (88.60%)

- **Property 3:** Western Brisbane, Queensland, 2020 for $349,000

  Today's value: $690,000 (97.71%)

- **Property 4:** Bendigo, Victoria, 2020 for $360,000

  Today's value: $500,000 (38.89%)

- **Property 5:** Adelaide, 2021 for $380,000

  Today's value: $710,000 (86.84%)

Total portfolio value today: $3.140 million and growing
Total equity growth: $1.289 million and growing

MICHAEL THOMAS – INVESTORKIT CLIENT

Michael is a busy business owner based in Sydney who began his property investment journey in his late 20s. With our guidance, he transitioned from owning one investment property to successfully building a diverse 11-property portfolio across five states with a total value of over $12.865 million – all by the time he hit his early 30s. Michael is a true testament to how hard work pays off when you do your due diligence, trust the right experts and apply the frameworks. He's built an eight-figure portfolio in just a few years and is now set up for life.

Before

Michael had big dreams of building wealth through property. Before we met him, he was working in the automotive industry buying and selling vehicles. He never had full-time employment until he was 25, but he'd bought his first investment property through another buyer's agent.

He joined InvestorKit in 2020, deciding that to expand his portfolio and start working towards his long-term goals, he needed expert guidance and strategic decision-making. He liked our data-driven approach too, rather than opinions, hype and oversimplification.

The process

We started by investing in foundational residential properties in major cities. Our strategy included properties across five states, ensuring his portfolio was balanced, resilient and primed for growth.

From the beginning, Michael was committed to thorough due diligence. He built a team of experts around him, recognising that going solo would have meant more time required and a higher risk of making costly mistakes, short-changing the growth of his portfolio.

Michael made sure that every asset was carefully assessed to ensure it aligned with his goals and met his high-growth, high-yield criteria. We ensured every acquisition added diversity and momentum to his portfolio, balancing risk and reward while optimising market timing. Finally, every property was purchased at the right price, ensuring Michael avoided overpaying and maximised returns from the outset.

Over time, he diversified into momentum properties in major regional centres and transitioned into commercial investments as his portfolio and financial position matured. Rather than letting money sit idle in his bank account, he channelled his profits into high-growth then higher cashflow assets, demonstrating a proactive and strategic approach to wealth building. He also invested without hesitation, despite external challenges like the pandemic, border closures, global uncertainty and rising interest rates. This enabled him to move forward guided by us, while others waited on the sidelines.

The result

During our journey together, Michael transitioned from an employee to being self- employed running a wholesale and retail automotive business. His earnings increased, but he remained disciplined with his finances and understood the importance of building wealth alongside his business. His motivation remains to enjoy abundance by leveraging his strong financial position and continuing to build his portfolio while he grows his successful business.

Today, Michael's portfolio comprises seven residential and four commercial properties with a value of $12.865 million across five states, ensuring resilience and reduced risk.

Michael's story exemplifies the power of strategic investing and trusting the right experts. By combining business acumen with financial discipline, he has achieved a level of success most investors can only aspire to.

Michael's property journey

- **Property 1 (his own purchase):** Loganholme, Brisbane, 2020 for $307,500

  Today's value: $650,000 (111.38%)

- **Property 2:** Wynnum West, Brisbane, 2021 for $560,000

  Today's value: $1.02 million (82.43%)

- **Property 3:** Hallett Cove, Adelaide, 2021 for $555,000

  Today's value: $830,000 (49.55%)

- **Property 4:** Killarney Vale, New South Wales, 2021 for $950,000

  Today's value: $1.1 million (15.79%)

- **Property 5:** Bargara, Queensland, 2022 for $720,000

  Today's value: $950,000 (31.95%)

- **Property 6:** Pakenham, Victoria, 2023 for $706,000

  Today's value: $770,000 (9.07%)

- **Property 7:** Harrington Park, New South Wales, 2024 for $1.165 million

  Today's value: $1.5 million (28.76%) ($250,000 renovation)

  (Partially supported by InvestorKit: Michael's owner-occupied home)

- **Property 8:** Rockingham, Western Australia, 2024 for $1.7 million (commercial)

  Net Yield: 7.15%

  Property & Lease: Industrial, 4.5 years remaining with 3.5% annual increases.

- **Property 9:** Queanbeyan West, New South Wales, 2024 for $1.1 million (commercial)

  Net Yield: 5.91%

  Property & Lease: Medical, four years remaining with another four-year option, 3.5%+ annual increases

- **Property 10:** Mooroopna, Victoria, 2024 for $500,000 (commercial)

  Net Yield: 6.25%

  Property & Lease: Medical, four years remaining with another four-year option, 3.5%+ annual increases

- **Property 11:** South Gladstone, Queensland, 2024 for $2.745 million (commercial)

  Net Yield: 9.07%

  Property & Lease: Mixed-use WALE 2.5 years with CPI increases across 10x tenancies

Further to the above, at the time of writing this book we have exchanged on two × more commercial properties for Michael that have not been included in overall figures.

TL:DR 3 TIPS

When you've already put in a lot of effort applying the right framework to your purchase, it can be a hard pill to swallow realising that there's a final step towards acquisition: due diligence. But trust me, apply these three parts when you think you've found the right suburb or property to invest in and this process will ensure you make the best decision for you and your portfolio, setting you up for life.

Simply:

1. follow the 20-point due diligence checklist
2. look at comparable sales
3. consider your cashflow analysis and portfolio fit.

* * *

To recap, you've now unlearned the myths, learnt the right property fundamentals, applied the three market categorisations and are ready to acquire your property. Don't skip due diligence and hope for the best because you think you know your local area or the investment opportunity – our process is data-driven and tried and true, to take away all of the guesswork.

Stick with this and you'll be well on your way to achieving your dreams!

Grab Your Free Bonus Resources!

Enjoying the book? Head to
www.investorkit.com.au/book-resources
to unlock your exclusive bonus materials, tools, indicators and templates designed to help you take action and get results.

Don't miss out – they're free and ready for you now!

EPILOGUE

Throughout the pages of this book, I've taken you on an incredible journey of the InvestorKit property systems and processes. Well done for making it through to the other side!

First, we looked at mythbusting, and how we're all fed mistruths about the property market through our families, the media, our work or simply our own beliefs. This was about going back to basics, exposing the property lies and unlearning what you know or think you know. In this part, I presented the most popular myths and then proved why they're wrong – by looking at the numbers.

Next, we looked at the property fundamentals. This was about rebuilding your knowledge and learning a system that reflects the market accurately, starting with the three core drivers of the property market – demand, supply and confidence – and the 26 metrics or indicators that reveal what is really happening.

Then, it was time to put your new knowledge to the test. I presented the key frameworks I use to apply the metrics when I'm making decisions to yield the best results. Instead of relying on a property clock, which is commonly referred to in the media, I use spider charts. These illustrate three market cycles: early-adopter, hotspot and second-wind. They evolve the thinking of the property fundamentals in a practical way, enabling you to apply the spider charts to a property you're interested in to see which cycle it fits into, so you can accurately 'predict' where to invest because you can see what it's expected to do in the future. We assess every property we consider purchasing for our clients against the spider charts, and now you can too.

Finally, I took you to the next step of acquiring your property and how you can avoid making costly mistakes by applying thorough due diligence. We use a 20-point checklist to find properties with high appeal, high resale value and high streams of growth and income. And that's what we all want out of property investing, isn't it?!

Of course, one of the incredible aspects of successful property investing is that there's no one-size-fits-all solution. Markets keep changing, economies keep evolving and governments keep swinging, creating ever-shifting goalposts that can be hard to keep up with. For me, this is what's exciting. There are so many opportunities, and so much never-ending data!

While it's our goal to be across these movements so you don't have to, in this book hopefully I have enlightened you in the way we work with the tools and knowledge so that you feel better educated. If you already have a portfolio, I hope this opens new pathways to thinking about property investing, grounded in a systematic, factual and informed approach designed to help you build wealth over the long term. No shonky property schemes here!

Of course, your danger is analysis paralysis, which you will have read about in some of our case studies. People like Lorna, whose first investment went so badly she lost confidence to try again. Or our client Daniel, who had successfully bought properties on his own but was afraid of making another costly mistake or having FOMO. Both have now set themselves up for life, and we couldn't be happier for them.

Like our incredible clients, you must be prepared to put in the work; there are no shortcuts. It's easy to be put off by only hearing about the failures, but we know what works – facts and data get consistently great results. Being better informed means being less reactive to property media and noise and a growing confidence to trust the process.

Your journey through this book may be finishing, but hopefully the experience has opened up a whole new way of thinking for you. It did for me when I realised that unlocking data was the key to success in the property market, and I hope it will for you too.

With your new learnings and an open mind, you can now unlock some fantastic opportunities. Your knowledge will take you all over Australia with property investments you may never have contemplated for you and your family. You'll focus on a plan that you can control rather than the other way around, with an expert team to implement it.

I can't wait to see you thrive in ways you only dreamed of. Remember to access all the resources in this book, and feel free to connect with us and subscribe to our YouTube channel (InvestorKit) and newsletter.

Happy dreaming, buying and thriving!

ABOUT THE AUTHOR

Arjun Paliwal built his $20+ million property portfolio the hard way: by questioning everything, following the numbers, and never settling for the status quo. After surviving a life-threatening heart condition in his early 30s, Arjun doubled down on his mission to help everyday Australians build wealth through intentional, evidence-based investing. Today, as the Founder and Head of Research at InvestorKit, he leads one of Australia's fastest-growing and most awarded property research and wealth creation agencies. With more than 2000 properties purchased, over $1B+ in transactions and over $500 million in equity growth created for clients, Arjun is proof that curiosity, courage and data can change your life.

- INVESTORKIT.COM.AU
- @INVESTORKIT
- @INVESTORKIT
- FACEBOOK.COM/INVESTORKIT

AUDIOBOOK

Great news! *Driving The Data* is also available in audio format.

Jump onto your favourite audiobook platform now and check it out.

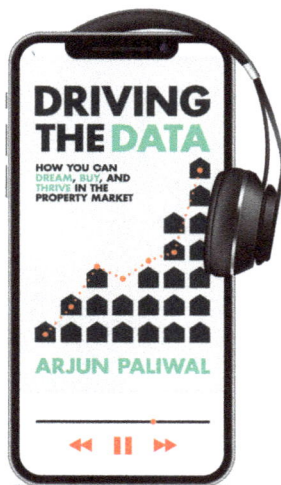

www.ingramcontent.com/pod-product-compliance
Lightning Source LLC
Chambersburg PA
CBHW040851210326
41597CB00029B/4804